D0850816

Altered

Environments

The Outer Banks of North Carolina

Text by **Jeffrey Pompe**

Photographs by **Kathleen Pompe**

The University of South Carolina Press

Published by the University of South Carolina Press
Columbia, South Carolina 29208

www.sc.edu/uscpress

Manufactured in the United States of America

19 18 17 16 15 14 13 12 11 10   10 9 8 7 6 5 4 3 2 1

Library of Congress Cataloging-in-Publication Data

Pompe, Jeffrey J., 1951–
  Altered environments : the Outer Banks of North Carolina / text by
Jeffrey Pompe ; photographs by Kathleen Pompe.
      p. cm.
  Includes bibliographical references and index.
  ISBN 978-1-57003-923-2 (cloth : alk. paper)
  1. Outer Banks (N.C.)—Environmental conditions. 2. Outer
Banks(N.C.)—History. 3. Outer Banks (N.C.)—Pictorial works. 4. Landscape
changes—North Carolina—Outer Banks—History. 5. Natural history—North
Carolina—Outer Banks. 6. Nature—Effect of human beings on—North
Carolina—Outer Banks—History. 7. Coastal ecology—North Carolina—Outer
Banks—History. 8. Human ecology—North Carolina—Outer Banks—History.
9. Social change—North Carolina—Outer Banks—History. 10. Outer Banks
(N.C.)—Social conditions. I. Pompe, Kathleen. II. Title.
  GE155.N8P66 2010
  304.209756'1—dc22
                                    2010005638

. . . .

. . . .

Dedicated to those who always return to places at the edge of the sea.
May each find new hope.

. . . .

Contents

Illustrations

Table

Preface

Our fascination with the Outer Banks began when we first visited the islands twenty years ago. As we revisited the Outer Banks over the years, we soon recognized that the interaction between nature and humankind created a narrative that invited reflection and study. While nature's forces make the Outer Banks and other barrier islands some of the most rapidly changing places in the world, humankind's activities alter the islands as well. In *Altered Environments* we explore this complex interaction between humankind and nature and examine the forces that have created an environment so different from the Outer Banks of only a few decades ago.

When we first learned of the 1930s dune-construction project of the Civilian Conservation Corps (CCC), we recognized a historical demarcation that altered life on the Outer Banks from what came before. Constructing a wall of dunes along 125 miles of shoreline changed the Outer Banks in many ways. Most important, the project ushered the area into the last half of the twentieth century, when Americans would increasingly coveted the shore. In *Altered Environments* our goal is to provide a historical perspective of how nature and humankind have shaped this unique area and to interpret the interaction between humankind and the changeable barrier-island environment. After all, things are not always what they seem. Indeed the 1930s CCC project sounded a theme that resonates throughout Outer Banks history: alterations of the islands may create unexpected and unforeseen consequences.

We introduce the reader to the Outer Banks environment and the concerns that many barrier-island communities must address. In general, however, we consider social, environmental, and economic issues that are relevant to many twenty-first-century coastal areas. Coastal communities face unique problems, such as natural disasters and rising sea levels, and in recent decades the rapid growth in coastal population has exacerbated many of the problems. We examine the sources of coastal-area problems and consider actions that may encourage sustainable communities in such locations.

The Outer Banks and other coastal areas are changeable but resilient lands that invite many questions worthy of investigation. We believe that *Altered Environments* will be of interest to the casual Outer Banks visitor who is curious about his or her environs and also to those who wish to understand the difficult choices faced by residents, business owners, coastal managers, and others who live along the U.S. coastline. With the increasing rate of sea-level rise and growing numbers of residents and visitors, the challenges for coastal communities will be greater than ever before.

The geology, history, and culture of the distinctive islands that form the Outer Banks have brought us back time and time again to this land surrounded by the sea. We hope some of our fascination is shared with the readers of *Altered Environments*. Authors from other disciplines, such as history and geology, provide greater detail and analysis of individual topics that we introduce. For those interested in more in-depth studies of specific issues, our bibliography provides information on some of the authors who have given us insight into the changing nature of the Outer Banks.

For their generous support that contributed to the completion of this project, we are grateful to the following: members of the administration of Francis Marion University, who have consistently encouraged our endeavors in many ways, including a joint sabbatical that allowed the initial research for this project; Alexander Moore, our editor, who persevered and was enthusiastic about the project throughout its development; the many others at the University of South Carolina Press who have been excellent colleagues; Brad Jordan at Phoenix Design, who provided the illustrations; Jim and Penny for their Outer Banks hospitality; Winn Dough and Stuart Parks at the Outer Banks History Center; Steve Harrison and Jason Powell with the Natural Parks Service; and three anonymous readers who suggested improvements.

Altered Environments

The Outer Banks

One

A Place Created by Change

There is nothing permanent except change.

Heraclitus

Not much wider than 3 miles at the broadest place and barely 100 yards at the narrowest point, the Outer Banks consists of a succession of narrow islands that shelter the North Carolina mainland from the sea for more than 175 miles. At the northernmost section of the Outer Banks, Currituck Banks and Bodie Island, which are connected, arc southeasterly for 55 miles before ending at Oregon Inlet. This northernmost section of the Outer Banks is not technically an island because it is connected to Cape Henry, Virginia. Beyond Oregon Inlet a series of five islands, separated by inlets, composes the remaining Outer Banks. Pea and Hatteras islands (which are connected) turn southerly for 60 miles until Cape Hatteras, where the land makes a dramatic right-angle turn at Cape Point. The remainder of Hatteras Island, and the islands of Ocracoke, Portsmouth, and Core Banks, swing southwesterly for 48 miles before culminating at Cape Lookout. Nine-mile-long Shackleford Banks lies perpendicular to Core Banks, jutting in toward the mainland until cut off by Beaufort Inlet.

Five inlets—Oregon, Hatteras, Ocracoke, Drum, and Barden—separate the islands from each other. The inlets, which are not stable, can be difficult to navigate because they continually shift and sometimes even close completely. Ocracoke is the only inlet currently open that was open during the sixteenth century when Europeans first explored the Outer Banks.

The islands of the Outer Banks are a few of the nearly three hundred barrier islands that buffer the Atlantic Ocean and Gulf of Mexico coastlines.[1] The shallow sounds that separate the Outer Banks from the mainland are twenty to forty miles wide. The five broad sounds—Albemarle, Pamlico, Currituck, Roanoke, and Core—cover more than three thousand square miles and separate the Outer Banks from the mainland much more than most barrier islands do. For many barrier islands, often a bridge over a waterway makes the connection between the mainland and an island so simply that one does not recognize that the mainland now lies behind. However, on the Outer Banks the wide expanse of water between the mainland and islands creates the sense of being far out at sea. Often as a boater crosses one of the sounds, land is not visible; low-lying land is visible only from at least twenty miles away because of the earth's curvature. Although expansive, the sounds are so shallow that only small craft can travel over them. For example, the average depth of Pamlico and Core sounds is twelve and one-half feet and four feet respectively.

Besides separating the islands from the mainland, sounds are valuable natural resources, providing an important nursery for fish and other marine life and recreational benefits for humans. Every day as much as fifteen billion gallons of freshwater from North Carolina's rivers flow into the sounds, mixing with ocean water that flows through the inlets. This mix of fresh and salt waters is just the right combination for a maritime nursery that allows shrimp, blue crab, flounder, and many other species of fish to spawn and mature in the protected waters before heading to the open seas. In addition the sounds moderate the temperature on the Outer Banks, creating cooler summers and warmer winters than those on the mainland. The sound waters absorb heat in the summer (moderating temperatures to between seventy and eighty-two degrees) and give off heat in the winter (moderating temperatures to between forty-three and fifty-six degrees).

Sand dunes are the highest topographical features on the Outer Banks, which is predominantly flat. Although most sand dunes are no more than 10 to 12 feet tall, there are a few exceptions, such as Jockey's Ridge, which towers 110 feet above the sea. Jockey's Ridge, which is constantly moving, is encroaching on a maritime forest and nearby homes. Although natural forces build sand dunes, in some places on the Outer Banks humankind has contributed. Workers employed by the Civilian Conservation Corps (CCC) built more than 100 miles of artificial sand dunes along the Outer Banks shoreline in the 1930s.

The Gulf Stream, a river of water flowing clockwise past the coasts of the United States, Europe, and Africa, shapes life on the Outer Banks. The Gulf Stream's warm water helps moderate temperatures along the Carolinas. At Cape Point, where Hatteras Island makes a sharp right-angle turn, land is closer to the Gulf Stream than anyplace north of South Florida. At this point the Gulf Stream turns away from the North American coast and moves out to sea.

The combination of winds, currents, inlets, and shoals has created treacherous conditions for ships that attempt to navigate the Outer Banks. The collision of two powerful currents—the warm Gulf Stream traveling northerly and Arctic currents (known as the Virginia Coastal Drift) traveling

In 1975 a state park was created at Jockey's Ridge, the largest naturally formed sand dune in the eastern United States. Each year more than one million visitors enjoy the park.

The *Laura Barnes,* a four-masted wooden schooner that wrecked on Coquina Beach in 1921, one of many ships claimed along the dangerous Outer Banks shoreline. This photograph was taken in 1957. Courtesy of the National Park Service, Cape Hatteras National Seashore

southerly—creates Diamond Shoals, which has been responsible for many shipwrecks over the years. The Gulf Stream slows southbound ships and forces them near the shore and shoals, while nearshore currents slow northbound ships. Winds blowing from both the southwest and northeast create further difficulties for ships attempting to round the capes. The moniker "Graveyard of the Atlantic" was well earned by the Outer Banks shoreline. The conditions along the Outer Banks were responsible for almost three hundred shipwrecks between 1841 and 1930 and almost four hundred known wrecks in total. More ships rest on the ocean bottom here than any other place along the U.S. East Coast.

Formation of the Outer Banks

The geologic processes of mountain formation and erosion took millions of years to shape the coastline. The forces of seismic activity, climatic conditions, and sea-level change created coastlines slowly but dramatically. The forces began shaping the current coastline two hundred million years ago, when the continental landmasses that formed the single supercontinent Pangea began to separate and drift apart. As the twelve lithospheric plates—six bearing continents and six bearing oceans—drifted on a sea of molten material known as asthenosphere, some plates converged and produced folding and mountain building. The force and power of the convergence compressed the continents to create mountains. The collision of two similar ancient tectonic plates, the ancestral North American and ancestral Atlantic, created the Appalachian Mountains. Millions of years of erosion moved the sediment that formed the broad continental shelf and the many barrier islands along the East Coast from the Appalachians to the coastline.

Although the processes that form shorelines have been at work for millions of years, in their present form the Outer Banks and other barrier islands developed relatively recently. Only twenty thousand years ago, at the end of the last ice age, the North American coastline was much different than it is today. Sea level was four hundred feet lower, and the landmass was much larger. The North Carolina coast was fifty to seventy-five miles seaward of today's coastline, and no barrier islands guarded the North Carolina mainland.[2] Over thousands of years, as rising temperatures melted the glacial ice sheet, sea level rose rapidly—by as much as an inch per decade—inundating coastal areas. However, around six thousand years ago glacial melting slowed, and sea level began to rise at a slower rate—about one-eighth of an inch per decade.

Conditions were eventually right for the Outer Banks and other barrier islands along the Atlantic and gulf coasts to form. The slowdown in sea

Sea oats and American beach grass, which are among the plants closest to the shore, hold sand in place against the wind and waves and help to stabilize Outer Banks shorelines.

level rise allowed coastlines to form and sand to accumulate along the United States coastline from New England to Texas. The frequent hurricanes and northeasters along the southeastern United States coastline created storm surges that drove grains of sand above the normal tidal range and eventually formed sandbars along the North Carolina mainland. A large supply of nearby sand, perhaps from offshore, provided the construction material necessary to form the islands.[3]

However, the loose sand granules that formed the sandbars would continue to move (as they do in the desert), and the barrier islands would be much less hospitable, if there were no vegetation to stabilize the sand. Sea oats and American beach grass were the first plants to establish residence and take hold, but they did not begin until after the rains reduced the salt content in the sand. The grasses slowed the wind velocity and caused blowing sand to be deposited in the grass. Other plants and flotsam trapped additional sand, and gradually sand accumulated and formed dunes parallel to the shore. Eventually other plants such as bayberry and beach pea added nitrates, which are necessary for other vegetation, to the sand. As the dunes stabilized and the soil developed, trees such as cedars, pines, and live oaks colonized the expanding ribbons of sand, creating a maritime forest in many places. At this point the topography of today's Outer Banks became recognizable. Wildlife such as birds, deer, squirrels, rabbits, opossums, and reptiles soon populated the land. This completed the neighborhood until humans (Native Americans were the first) arrived, probably not far behind the wildlife.

Although geologists offer other theories that explain the formation of the Outer Banks, all agree that barrier islands are young—less than ten thousand years old. On a planet with rocks more than four billion years old, barrier islands are mere babes. When considering rocks that are millions and even billions of years old, the geology of the Outer Banks may appear almost imperceptible for its briefness. To put this in perspective, there is a five-thousand-year-old bristlecone pine tree surviving in California that is almost as old as the Outer Banks.

Life on the Outer Banks

Plants are important to the barrier-island ecosystem because they immo-bilize sand and create some island stability. Surprisingly the sand on the Outer Banks can provide an excellent medium for the more than one hun-dred varieties of flowering plants that populate the Outer Banks. Distinct communities of plants colonize particular locations. Sea oats, American beach grass, and other dune plants that tolerate salt spray and sand burial are nearest the ocean. Beyond the grasses, in areas protected by the dune field, shrubs such as goldenrod, yaupon, wax myrtle, and bayberry flour-ish. Farther inland the forest zone comprises dogwoods, loblolly pines, and live oaks. The sea winds and salt spray shape the vegetation near the ocean. The windblown salt spray stunts tree growth and causes the branches to grow toward the west away from the ocean wind.

Although most vegetation along the Outer Banks is low to the sand, maritime forests, which are areas of trees, plants, and dense underbrush, provide some variation and are the most stable places on the islands. Three forests—Shackelford, Buxton Woods, and Nags Head Woods—have not been developed and are prime examples of maritime forests. Nags Head Woods, which is more than fifty thousand years old, has existed much longer than any other Outer Banks forest and, in fact, existed on the old mainland before the postglacial sea-level rise inundated the coastal plain and formed the Outer Banks.[4] The woods are a portion of the mainland that existed before the ocean rose. The Nature Conservancy preserves Nags Head Woods, which is a unique feature of the Outer Banks ecosystem. Buxton Woods, which is no older than six thousand years, expands over a series of high dune ridges, called relict dunes. Relict dunes are the rem-nants of an ancient shoreline.

Many common and some unique species of animals inhabit the Outer Banks. Near Cape Hatteras, which is the dividing area between the southern

To get to the community of Carova, the northernmost development of the
Outer Banks, residents and visitors must drive along the shoreline.

and northern Atlantic Ocean, the mix of coastal currents and water temperatures creates favorable conditions for an abundance of fish and sea-
birds. Small vertebrates such as raccoons, rabbits, and rice rats as well as
numerous species of amphibians and reptiles are among the common animal life. Fowler's toads, tree toads, diamondback terrapins, and box turtles
make the Core Banks home, and threatened loggerhead turtles nest on the
beaches in the spring and early summer.

Humans have lived on the Outer Banks for at least three thousand
years and may have visited there even earlier. However, humans have populated the Outer Banks in significant numbers only in the past century;
even today, following the development of infrastructure and the increased
popularity of coastal areas, the year-round population is only about fifty-
seven thousand. Today ferries, bridges, and paved roads connect most parts
of the Outer Banks, which comprise parts of the four North Carolina counties of Currituck, Dare, Hyde, and Carteret. Although no roads exist for the
twenty-five miles from the Virginia border south to the town of Corolla,
four-wheel-drive vehicles can traverse the beach sand, and a community
has developed in this roadless section. State Highway 12 runs from Corolla
south past the towns of Kitty Hawk and Nags Head and connects Bodie
and Hatteras islands. A ferry ride across Hatteras Inlet interrupts the highway before it continues and then concludes at Ocracoke village, where
another ferry connects Ocracoke to Cedar Island and the mainland.

Although economic development has created thriving tourist communities along the Outer Banks, some sections are still undeveloped and other

areas can be reached only by boat. Two areas designated as national sea-
shores protect 128 miles of undeveloped shoreline from development: 70
miles at Cape Hatteras and 58 miles at Cape Lookout that include Portsmouth Island, Core Banks, and Shackleford Banks. Because the federal
government owns the land, Cape Lookout National Seashore is hardly developed; no roads traverse the islands, and no bridges or ferries connect
them to the mainland.

Jared Diamond summarizes the subject of his book *Guns, Germs, and Steel*
in one sentence: "History followed different courses for different peoples
because of differences among people's environments, not because of biological differences among peoples themselves."[5] Diamond explains that environmental differences led to the Europeans' ability to conquer the Mayans,
Aztecs, and others in the "New World" even though the Native Americans
had a large advantage in numbers as well as the incentive of defending
their homeland. Europeans were victorious because of the weapons and
diseases they inflicted on the "New World"—weapons and diseases for
which native populations had no defense. According to Diamond, environmental factors led to the development of these tools of destruction. For
example geographical barriers created conditions that led to the domesti-
cation of animals in Europe, which eventually led to the development of the
technology that allowed the Europeans to create superior weapons.

However, just as the environment shapes human history, humans shape
environments, as George Marsh asserted almost one and one-half centuries
ago in his book *Man and Nature*. Marsh, who described how activities
such as deforestation and overgrazing had changed environments, observed
that humankind's alterations of natural systems contributed to the fall of
empires and the ruination of whole regions.

The observations of Diamond and Marsh are especially applicable to the
Outer Banks, where humankind, sea, and sand are so intertwined. Especially in the last half of the twentieth century, as humankind has rushed
to the shore, rapid development of coastal areas has created many changes
to the barrier-island environment. Communities on the Outer Banks may
seem like other communities built on solid ground; the shopping malls,
residences, and businesses on the Outer Banks are similar to those in
other communities. However, the sea and wind that constantly rearrange
the sands on which the Outer Banks communities are built make barrier
islands some of the most changeable places on earth. Extreme weather
events such as hurricanes and northeasters, which are common on the
Outer Banks, can rapidly alter the landscape.

waves and wind, sand dunes are important reservoirs that may provide replacement beach sand that is lost during storms. Dunes are not impenetrable defenses because overwash, which occurs when waves wash sand over the dunes onto the island or into the sound behind the island, can breach them. In addition dunes are mobile features that can sometimes create problems by migrating over roads, houses, and even whole communities. The barrier flat is a wide plain that can support grasslands, shrub thickets, or woodlands.

Although sand appears to be at the mercy of the elements, plants such as sea oats and beach grass, which find the sandy soil a welcome home, can stabilize the sand for a time. The plants, which trap sand and help to build dunes, provide natural protection for the Outer Banks. Recognizing the value of vegetation on shorelines, governments pass laws to protect the plants. Christian III, king of Denmark, passed one of the earliest laws to protect plants on dunes in the 1500s.[5]

Sand Shifters

Breaking waves and ocean currents are the principal movers of beach sand. A wave is a disturbance that transfers energy through a medium in such a way that the medium itself remains intact after the wave has passed. The process is similar to the effects witnessed when one throws a stone into a pond.[6] Throwing a stone into a pond injects energy into a portion of the pond. The concentric circles radiating outward transfer the initial energy to the pond's shoreline, creating a small amount of erosion. When the pond calms down, it is the same as before the stone's insertion, but the shoreline is changed. Each ocean wave, whether a mild ripple or a hurricane-force-driven wave, moves some sand and changes the beach. Each one of the eight thousand waves that collide with the beach daily can hurl thousands of tons of water onto the shore. A single four-foot-high breaking wave strikes the shore with 65,600 foot-pounds, or 33 foot-tons, of energy.[7]

Most waves that reach the shoreline were created out at sea by a breeze blowing over the water surface. The breeze, which begins when the sun warms the air, transfers energy to the waves. Two factors determine a wave's strength: the fetch, which is the distance the wave travels without meeting an obstacle; and the strength of the wind. The longer the fetch and the stronger the wind, the bigger is the wave. Large storms can create long period waves known as swells that can travel half the distance around the world. The bigger a wave gets, the more efficiently it absorbs additional energy.

As waves approach the beach, they strike the ocean floor, releasing their stored energy and causing sand movement in the surf zone. When a

Despite the transitory nature of barrier islands and the threat of extreme weather, many barrier islands have become some of the most densely populated places in the country. The population growth has exacerbated the problems that are inevitable on an island. The alluring but changeable shoreline can threaten the property and security of those who live on and visit barrier islands. Often for this reason humans alter the coastal environment to make the land more suitable for development and to create greater stability. Unfortunately human actions, which are not always successful, often do more harm than good. Some of the changes have caused problems such as beach erosion, water pollution, and loss of wildlife habitat.

Many love the Outer Banks, but the inspiration that transports each one to the islands varies. Families may have ties to the land; some hope to find a new beginning; others are drawn to the wildness, isolation, and raw beauty; some may be searching for a brief respite from the cares and troubles of daily life. However, all who love the Outer Banks must love movement and change, for the seashore, and especially the seashore of a barrier island, is a place of unwavering restlessness. The human fascination with the transformable sea must explain in part why so many choose to be at the shore. Yet those who choose to live on a barrier island must learn to adapt to an island environment that will not be still.

In order to protect the shorelines that so many enjoy, society must understand the interaction between humans and nature on barrier islands. With further development expected on the Outer Banks, and in other coastal areas, society must consider how growth has affected this valuable natural resource and what may lie ahead. In Altered Environments we examine the changes that nature and humans create on the Outer Banks, and coastal communities in general, and the outcomes of those changes.

Two

Change by Nature

Look abroad thro' Nature's range. Nature's mighty law is change.

Robert Burns

Before humans ever set foot on the Outer Banks, nature's forces made change an integral part of the physical environment. The persistent winds and enormous energy released by breaking waves make the ocean coastline one of the fastest changing places on earth. The forces of sea and wind alter the coastal environment from moment to moment, building up some shorelines and wearing away others; cutting a new inlet here, removing the tip of an island there. Each ocean wave that reaches the land rearranges the shoreline, adding or subtracting countless grains of sand. Every ocean breeze stirs additional grains, sometimes encouraging with a gentle nudge and other times issuing a blast that flings sand into a stinging swarm.

The movement of sand is part of the natural rhythm of a shore-line environment that has adapted to the vagaries of nature. However, as one muses over the shoreline's kaleidoscopic patterns, one might imagine some additional purpose to the manipulations of sand by sea and wind. Perhaps nature composes a sequence of sand granules that satisfies a momentary beach-front cosmic equation that explains the purpose of the universe, the "unified theory" sought by physicists. In the next moment nature erases the solution and then immediately modulates the theme to a new key. Whatever cosmic mysteries might be revealed on the mesmerizing shoreline, one must appreciate the fascinating processes that compose the beach.

The Nature of Sand

A medium-sized grain of sand, about the size of a grain of table salt, is generally from one and one-sixteenth to two millimeters in diameter.[1] Although size may vary from beach to beach, at any particular area of a beach the sand grains are similar in size. This is because the waves, practicing what is known as "good sorting," arrange sediment particles so that at any one place the particles are about the same size. Despite the sorting,

each grain of sand, if closely examined, is slightly different from its neighbor, much as each snowflake is unique. Such a variety of shapes is an astounding degree of inventiveness because beach sand, which is mostly quartz, is one of the commonest minerals on the planet. Quartz, or silicon dioxide, is a colorless mineral that is hard and resistant to weathering. It is a good thing that quartz is so hard because each grain of sand endures a great deal of weathering over a lengthy existence. That grain of sand that crunches beneath your foot could tell a tale of the ages because that granule might be millions of years old.

Most of the sand on the Outer Banks probably began when weather, vegetation, and gravity combined to break granitic rocks from mountains into quartz and feldspar. Washed into a mountain stream by the rain, a grain of sand begins its journey from mountain to shore. The journey may be lengthy with many extended stops on the way. Before traveling far down the mountain, the granule might become trapped by the roots of a spruce pine, which might grow for one hundred years before being split in two by a bolt of lightning. Gradually dying and decaying, the tree feeds new life and eventually frees the grain of sand to continue its journey. Even if a grain of sand is not sidetracked, the process is lengthy. It takes the average river a million years to move a grain of sand one hundred miles closer to the sea.[2] For a grain of sand that began as part of North Carolina's Blue Ridge Mountains, the trip from beginning to end could easily last some three million years. Witness to the erosion of mountain peaks and the evolution of Homo sapiens, a grain of sand might be the ultimate chronicler of time.

Once on the beach a grain of sand does not rest but is always in motion, responding to the waves, currents, and winds that act upon it. Beaches, the most actively changing segment of barrier islands, are not stable but are in dynamic equilibrium, continually balancing among four elements: beach material (sand, shell fragments, silt, coral, and flotsam); energy (winds, waves, currents, and tides); sea level; and shape of the beach.[3] The balancing act is a wise survival tactic in the face of such energetic and potent forces. Rather than resisting storm waves, beaches absorb and dissipate wave force while strategically retreating. During a storm, for example the beach flattens out, exhausting the storm-wave energy over a broader area so that the shoreline suffers less harm. Following the storm the beach will return to its previous slope.

As ephemeral as a sand grain may appear, the grains of sand form make a unified beach, which is only a portion of the typical barrier island. Other zones include the dunes, maritime forest, flats, and marshes.[4] primary and secondary sand dunes provide the principal defense against storm surge and erosion. Besides providing a temporary defense ag deep-sea swell enters shallow water, its leading edge slows and water piles up behind it. This makes the wave grow again. Therefore, although the wave is slowing, it is also growing taller, thus creating more potential change for the shoreline. There are three types of waves: spilling, plunging, and collapsing. Spilling and plunging waves move sand away from the beach, but collapsing waves add sand. Spilling and plunging breakers are much more common than collapsing breakers, and therefore beach erosion is more likely, other things constant, than beach accretion.

Waves usually meet the shore at an angle, creating a longshore current that moves sand parallel to the beach between the shoreline and the breaker zone of the waves. Longshore currents (also referred to as littoral drift) act like a shallow river channel that generally moves at ten to twenty centimeters per second, although a strong wind can increase the speed to one hundred centimeters per second. Although longshore currents often move sand back and forth along a beach, because waves approach the coast at different angles, over time there is a net movement of sand. Currents along the Outer Banks move parallel to the shore, sweeping sand in a southerly direction from the Virginia border to Cape Hatteras and then westerly as the Outer Banks veers west. Together wave action and longshore currents can move tons of sediment in a single day. Natural forces move five hundred thousand to one million cubic yards of sand each year along the Outer Banks.[8] That is equal to sixty-six thousand fully loaded dump trucks carrying about ten cubic yards of sand each.

Inlets, which connect the ocean to the sounds, are part of the sand-moving conveyer belt also. Inlets, which usually form during hurricanes or severe storms, are valuable release points for hurricane forces. As hurricanes approach the Outer Banks, the winds blowing from the southeast force storm-surge waters inland and up the estuaries. When the hurricane comes ashore, the winds, now blowing from the west, drive the water back toward the ocean in a rush. The powerful force of the water will cut a new inlet across low, narrow island areas when the water has no other place to go. The 1846 hurricane created two new inlets, Oregon and Hatteras, in this way. Recent hurricanes in 2003 and 2005 have opened Isabel Inlet and Ophelia Inlet respectively. The U.S. Army Corps of Engineers closed Ophelia Inlet within a little more than a month by using sand dredged from the Hatteras Inlet navigation channel.

Currents carry sediment through the inlets, forming tidal deltas. The sand forms ebb-tide deltas on the seaward side and flood-tide deltas on the sound side. Inlets help balance the sand equation for barrier islands by moving sand from the front of the beach to the sound side, where it builds up and helps with the process of island transgression. The motion of a landward-moving island, known as transgression, results in the complete island ecosystem rolling over itself and edging landward.[9] Geologists estimate that the Outer Banks' beach face translocates at a rate of five feet per year. Flood-tide deltas and overwash, which occurs when waves wash sand over dunes, are two ways that water moves sand across an island.

Inlets, which are not stable, sometimes can close completely or continue to migrate, as in the case of Oregon Inlet, which moves in a southerly direction.[10] The many factors that determine how inlets move, including wave energy, tidal range, and the amount of sand moving along the coast, combine to cause southward inlet migration along the Outer Banks.[11] In past years as many as nine inlets have been open at the same time on the Outer Banks, and since colonial times at least twenty-five different inlets have remained open long enough to be named.[12] Because inlets are dynamic (as is most everything in the barrier-island environment), they can be difficult to navigate. Sometimes humankind will attempt to stabilize an inlet or create a new inlet to maintain an open path between the sound and the ocean.

Waves, coastal currents, and tides create shoals by depositing sand along the shore. At Cape Point and Cape Lookout the shoals, which are shallower than the surrounding sea, stretch ten to fifteen miles seaward. At the capes the currents drag sand at dramatic angles to form the infamous Diamond Shoals and Cape Lookout Shoals. Many of the four hundred shipwrecks along the Outer Banks occurred on the shoals, which is a major reason why the Outer Banks was known as the Graveyard of the Atlantic. A minor mistake by a ship's captain could strand a ship on the shoals, where the waves would rip apart the ship.

Wind transports large amounts of sand in the island environment as well. The movement of sand by wind is known as "aeolian transport," after Aeolus, the ruler of the winds in Greek mythology. Fair-weather winds move more sand than do storm winds because storm winds occur infrequently and are often accompanied by rain. The wind patterns on the Outer Banks create unique dune formations some distance from the shore. From the Virginia border to Nags Head the Outer Banks run southeast to northwest at right angles to the direction of the prevailing winds, which blow predominantly from the northeast or southwest. Jockey's Ridge, the largest natural sand dune on the East Coast, may be the result of this bimodal wind field.[13] Northeast winds blow sand from the beach along the Jockey's Ridge dune face and deposit the sand on the southwest side. Southwest winds then blow sand back to the northeast side. The landmark 110-foot-high Jockey's Ridge sand dune is a popular spot for hang gliding and is not far from where the Wright brothers took their first flight. The combination

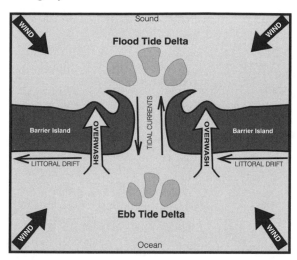

The water and sand that move through the inlets create flood-tide deltas on the sound side and ebb-tide deltas on the ocean side. Flood-tide deltas and overwash move sand toward land.

of storm winds, ocean swells, and high tides carries large amounts of sand from the beach across the island.

While waves and wind affect daily changes, sea-level rise alters barrier islands over a much lengthier period.[14] Sea level has fluctuated repeatedly over the last two million years as the planet has gone through cycles of warming and cooling. When the planet enters an ice age, huge sheets of ice trap masses of ocean water, and sea level falls. When global temperatures warm, sea levels rise as glaciers melt and discharge their water back into the sea. Sea level can change by more than 100 meters during the course of these changes. Rising sea level contributes to beach erosion, the deposition of sand in inlets, and the landward retreat of barrier islands. Sea level was 120 meters (300 feet) lower than today when the earth began the current warming trend twenty thousand years ago at the end of the last ice age. Twelve thousand years ago the retreat accelerated. Currently sea-level rise along the mid-Atlantic coast averages about a foot per century. Land subsidence, which can occur when oil or water is withdrawn from coastal areas, also can cause sea-level rise.

Although rising sea level is not a new phenomenon, climate change may cause sea levels to rise more quickly. A dramatic rise in carbon gases (primarily the result of burning fossil fuels) is creating a greenhouse effect around the planet, which is causing polar ice caps to melt. Some project that the resultant increase in global temperatures could melt enough ice cover in Greenland and Antarctica to increase sea level by two to three feet in the current century. The sea-level rise would cause flooding, salt-water intrusion into groundwater supplies, and the destruction of valuable

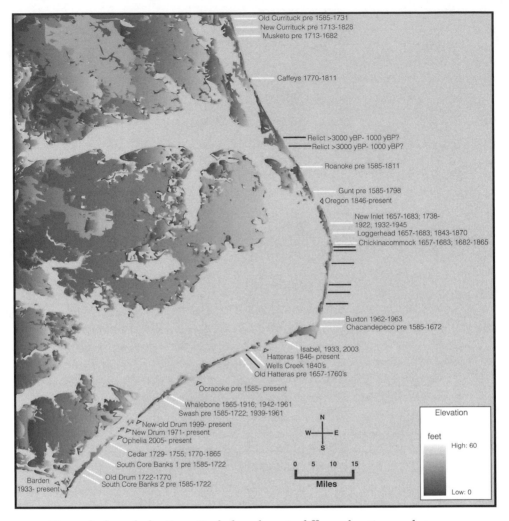

Old Currituck pre 1585-1731
New Currituck pre 1713-1828
Musketo pre 1713-1682

Caffeys 1770-1811

Relict >3000 yBP- 1000 yBP?
Relict >3000 yBP- 1000 yBP?

Roanoke pre 1585-1811

Gunt pre 1585-1798
Oregon 1846-present

New Inlet 1657-1683; 1738-
1922; 1932-1945
Loggerhead 1657-1683; 1843-1870
Chickinacommock 1657-1683; 1682-1865

Buxton 1962-1963
Chacandepeco pre 1585-1672

Isabel, 1933, 2003
Hatteras 1846- present
Wells Creek 1840's
Old Hatteras pre 1657-1760's

Ocracoke pre 1585- present

Whalebone 1865-1916; 1942-1961
Swash pre 1585-1722; 1939-1961
New-old Drum 1999- present
New Drum 1971- present
Ophelia 2005- present

Cedar 1729- 1755; 1770-1865
South Core Banks 1 pre 1585-1722

Barden
1933- present
Old Drum 1722-1770
South Core Banks 2 pre 1585-1722

N
W E
S

0   5   10   15
Miles

Elevation

feet
High: 60

Low: 0

Channels through the Outer Banks have been in different locations and at
different times. Black lines indicate previously undocumented inlets; white lines
indicate documented historical inlets; arrows point to present-day inlets. From
David J. Mallinson and others, *Past, Present and Future Inlets of the Outer Banks
Barrier Islands* (2008)

The creation of Jockey's Ridge State Park preserved 420 acres of *medaños* (sand dunes without vegetation). Visitors who hike to the top of the dunes have an excellent view of the Nags Head shoreline.

estuaries, property, and infrastructure. Because coastal processes occur over so narrow a range (all wave and current energy that affects the shore occurs within a vertical range of twenty meters on the shoreline), small changes in sea level can have significant impacts.[15]

Storms

Although winds and waves are constantly moving sand and altering shorelines, major storms can create sudden and dramatic changes. The destructiveness of hurricanes, which are the most powerful storms along the Atlantic coastline, is usually measured in human terms, such as the billions of dollars of property damage or the loss of lives. However, the damage to the coastal ecosystem can also be severe. The powerful storms can flood low-lying areas, breach dunes, destroy vegetation, and even create new inlets. Shore-line erosion can be extreme, as it was when Hurricane Hugo in 1989 produced some of the greatest short-term erosion of modern times along South Carolina shorelines.[16] Yet even hurricanes are an integral part of the barrier-island ecosystem. Hurricanes create habitat for nesting birds, replenish aquifers with fresh water, and flush waste out of waterways. Indeed, hurricanes help form barrier islands by moving the sand from the beach to the dunes and beyond.[17]

Although hurricanes may occur with an uncomfortable regularity, a great number of factors must be in alignment for these powerful storms to form. Consider the necessary conditions. Atlantic hurricanes brew off the African coast as the intense rays of the summer sun warm the ocean's surface. Evaporation and conduction transfer enormous amounts of heat and moisture into the atmosphere, providing the fuel required for the proper mix of meteorological conditions. The ocean must be at least eighty degrees to a depth of at least two hundred feet to sustain a high evaporation rate. Then surface winds must be converging from nearly opposite directions. This creates air circulation, reduces atmospheric pressure, and forces the moisture-laden air upward. In addition preexisting winds aloft must be relatively uniform in direction and intensity or the storm will be ripped apart. The air must be humid up to eighteen thousand feet, which infuses additional energy into the storm as moisture condenses. Additionally the atmospheric pressure must be higher at the top of the forming storm than surrounding regions; otherwise the surrounding air masses will snuff out the storm from the top. If all of these conditions are met, there is only weak surface wind circulation and the storm is not yet a hurricane but only a tropical disturbance. At this point there is still not much to be concerned with since only 10 percent of all tropical disturbances ever develop into hurricanes.[18]

The developing disturbance can create billowing clouds, scattered showers, and thunderstorms that grow to produce a low-pressure trough that begins to drift slowly westward. The trough may then develop into a tropical depression as barometric pressure drops and winds increase up to thirty-nine miles per hour (mph). The depression then develops into a tropical storm that can have winds up to seventy-four mph. Even at this stage the chances for a full-blown hurricane are not good. Of the twelve tropical storms spawned in an average year, only about half will grow into hurricanes.

The odds are clearly against the birth of hurricanes, but occasionally the devil looks after his own, as the proverb cautions. When the proper mix of conditions is met, the most dangerous and destructive of all storms is set loose. Meteorologists use the Saffir-Simpson scale to rate hurricane intensity. When a tropical storm attains wind velocity of 74 mph, it officially becomes a Category 1 hurricane. The most extreme, Category 5, hurricanes have speeds above 155 mph and storm surges more than eighteen feet. Fortunately, Category 5 hurricanes are infrequent. The only Category 5 hurricanes to make landfall in the United States in the twentieth century were

Northeasters such as the Ash Wednesday storm of 1962 can cause as much devastation as severe hurricanes. Photograph by Aycock Brown; courtesy of the Outer Banks History Center, Manteo, North Carolina

the 1935 Labor Day storm that pummeled the Florida Keys with winds around 200 mph; 1969's Camille, which smashed Biloxi, Mississippi, with winds more than 175 mph; and 1992's Hurricane Andrew.

Hurricanes strike between June and November each year, although most arise in August, September, and October. The Caribbean Islands, the eastern coast of Central America, the Gulf of Mexico coastline, and the eastern states from Florida to the Carolinas suffer the most from hurricanes. The frequency of Outer Banks hurricanes is as high as anyplace in the United States. While on average two hurricanes a year will strike the U.S. coastline anywhere between Texas and Maine, once every three to four years a hurricane will strike the North Carolina coast. However, there could be more than one hurricane in this interval or even multiple ones in a single year.

Northeasters, powerful storms that approach from the southwest generally but have winds that blow from the northeast and rotate counterclockwise, can wreak havoc on shorelines also. Second only to hurricanes in concentrated energy, northeasters can generate storm surge and waves that can cause even greater damage than hurricanes. These cyclonic storms, associated with intense low-pressure systems, occur more frequently, are much larger, and last longer than hurricanes. Most northeasters spread over a thousand miles and last for days. On average thirty northeasters develop each year, although fewer than one a year will cause serious damage.

One of the more damaging northeasters, the 1962 Ash Wednesday storm, produced waves more than thirty feet high and created millions of dollars in damage along the mid-Atlantic coast. High winds and waves from the storm tormented the northern Outer Banks for two days and created waves that broke through the dunes and covered much of the islands with two to four feet of water. The storm struck during spring tide, which exacerbated the damage.

Barrier islands are valuable landforms that are able to survive in places both beautiful and dangerous. Barrier islands shelter 34 percent of the United States coastline from the erosion and damage caused by wind and sea, including major sections of the U.S. eastern and gulf coasts. Nearly three hundred barrier islands protect more than twenty-seven hundred miles of coastline, buffer wave energy, and allow marshes and estuaries to form. This barrier against direct wave attack creates valuable habitats for plants, fishes, birds, and other animals, including many endangered species such as the whooping crane and the loggerhead sea turtle.

Barrier islands are able to endure continual assaults by wind, sea, and storms by yielding to the natural forces that constantly reshape shorelines. Recognizing the folly of confronting such powerful foes as wind and sea, a barrier island gives way, accommodating waves and sea-level rise by migrating toward the mainland. This is not surrender but rather a wise strategy that humans, who often try to confront powerful natural forces, might emulate. These mobile geological formations translocate from moment to moment and survive over the years by adapting to the forces of nature. Indeed, some five hundred years ago, when the first Europeans explorers mapped the Outer Banks, the beaches were almost a mile east of the present location.[19] Although the nature of sand is to move, the Outer Banks remains.

One can understand much about the physical forces that shape the shore, and yet what makes being at the beach unique and wonderful is something besides that knowledge. When one listens to a symphony, one does not hear the individual flute or violin but an integrated composition of rhythm, harmony, and melody. Just so at the seashore, one is treated to an orchestral banquet that satisfies all the senses. The hissing ocean, the caressing ocean breeze, the pungent salt mist, the patterns created by the waves—these are some of the elements that form a harmonious whole. One does not have to be a musician to appreciate a symphony nor a geologist to love the coastal environment. However, with careful attention one might discover a simple truth that, although difficult to express, speaks to the soul.

Three

Change by Humankind
. . . .

Man is everywhere a disturbing agent.

George Perkins Marsh
. . . .

In the mid–fourteenth century Europeans were enjoying a steady stream
of luxury goods such as spices, silks, and dyestuffs, which were produced
in Arab and Turkish lands. Many of the goods moved through Italian ports,
especially Genoa and Venice, where merchants grew wealthy by extract-
ing monopolistic fees from the trade. The Portuguese, chagrined at the
high prices for these luxury goods (and hoping to make some profit for
themselves), sent their fleet in search of a more direct trade route to the
countries that produced the goods. The failure of the first Portuguese sea
expeditions that sailed down the African coast in search of the route to the
luxury goods created a need for better navigational techniques. To produce
the navigational technology that would allow Europeans to sail to Asia in
search of spices and other riches, Prince Henry the Navigator of Portugal,
created a map-making school of navigation at Sagres, which is near the
most southwestern point of Europe. The scholars developed a navigational
technology that eventually brought Europeans, who were in search of a
shorter route to the Far East, to the Americas.

Europeans first discovered the North Carolina coast in 1521, during the
era of European exploration and conquest. Giovanni da Verrazano, an Italian leading a French expedition, recorded the first written account of the
Outer Banks in 1524. Verrazano, like many explorers, was seeking a westward passage to the Pacific and the Asian riches. When Verrazano saw no
shoreline west of the Outer Banks, he mistook the vast expanse of Pamlico
Sound for the "eastern sea" that bordered China. Verrazano did not attempt
to enter the sound, probably because shoals blocked his entrance. For the
next 150 years explorers mistakenly believed that a great sea stretched into
the middle of the North American continent. The error is evident on a 1582
map by Dr. John Dee that incorrectly locates a river that starts at the
Atlantic and connects to a lake that connects with another river that flows

to the Gulf of Mexico. John Farrer continued the misconception when he placed "Verrazano's Sea" on a 1651 map.

The thirst for trade, profits, and exploration led Europeans to the Outer Banks, and although generations of explorers continued the search for the fabled Northwest Passage, some began to settle and shape the land. Although the principal events that led to the current economy and environment on the Outer Banks occurred in the twentieth century, a brief review of some earlier history may be of interest.

An Introduction to Early Outer Banks History

Native Americans, the earliest inhabitants of the Outer Banks, visited the Outer Banks as early as 1000 C.E., although few would have lived on the Outer Banks year-round.[1] Most Native Americans would have preferred living on the mainland because the barrier islands bore the brunt of hurricanes and the winters were more pleasant in the security of inland forests. Although most tribes resided on the mainland, they would fish and hunt on the islands. The Croatans were the only Native Americans to live permanently on the Outer Banks.

Native American populations were small—probably no more than some hundreds—and there is no evidence that they significantly altered the environment. John White (one of the first Europeans to visit the Outer Banks), who drew and painted the flora, fauna, and Native Americans, provided a portrait of the Native Americans' life on the Outer Banks.[2] In 1585 White published this firsthand view of Native American life in *The Complete Drawings of John White*. The drawings of the first inhabitants, mostly Carolina Algonquians, show the inhabitants dressed in skins and living in small, scattered villages inhabited by between one hundred and two hundred people. The villages, which were always near some water body, comprised dwellings made from matting and bark and enclosed by palisades.

Native Americans used the abundant resources on the Outer Banks. They navigated the waters in shallow-draft dugout canoes catching finfish with crude nets (to catch large quantities) and sharpened poles (to spear small quantities). They also foraged for wild fruits, harvested shellfish, and hunted waterfowl. Archaeologists have found large mounds of discarded oyster shells that testify to Native Americans' presence on the Outer Banks, including one on Harkers Island that measures one hundred yards in diameter and is ten feet thick. Tribes (principally the Algonquians on the North Carolina coast) cleared and burned small sections of land to raise crops such as maize, sunflowers, pumpkins, and beans. However, because of the sandy soil on the Outer Banks most crops would have been raised on the mainland.

John White's 1585 drawing shows Native Americans using canoes, nets, and sharpened poles in the shallow sounds of the Outer Banks to catch the abundant fish. Courtesy of the University of North Carolina Library

After Verrazano's first visit, more than half a century passed before Europeans first tried to settle the Outer Banks. This first settlement attempt created one of the most intriguing historical events on the Outer Banks.

Although the French were the first Europeans to visit the Outer Banks, the English were the first to attempt a settlement. Sir Walter Raleigh planned the first permanent settlement in America, which was to be located on Roanoke Island. Raleigh saw an opportunity to establish a military base to harass Spanish ships and to explore the continent for gold and the passage to the East. In July 1584 a reconnaissance expedition landed, possibly at Core Banks, to claim the land for England. Under the command of Captains Philip Amadas and Arthur Barlowe, the two-vessel expedition spent six weeks that summer exploring and making contact with Native Americans. The group sailed through an inlet at Bodie Island to meet with the Roanoke Indians. On their return to England the two captains issued glowing reports of fertile land for fruits and crops, an abundance of game and fish, fine timber, skins and pearls, and friendly natives. The expedition sailed back to England with two willing Native Americans—Manteo and Wanchese—in order to demonstrate the natives' friendly nature.

Based on Amadas's and Barlowe's favorable reports, a second expedition, led by Sir Richard Grenville, left England in April 1585. Ralph Lane was named governor of the colony, which had 107 members, including the naturalist Thomas Hariot and the artist John White. White's drawings and Hariot's accounts of the land provide us with an important historical view of the Outer Banks as the first Europeans saw it. For example Hariot described the method used by Native Americans to grow some crops, especially maize and *uppowoc,* which the Spaniards referred to as tobacco. Hariot praised the uses of *uppowoc* not only for its health benefits but also for its importance in Native American ceremonies.

A third expedition, which left England in 1587 with 116 men, women, and children, planned to make a more permanent settlement. Roanoke Island, which is sheltered from the full force of ocean storms by Nags Head and Bodie Island, must have appeared to be a desirable location for a colony. Indeed John White, who was the governor of the settlement, proclaimed the Outer Banks to be "the goodliest and most pleasing territory of the world." Unfortunately for the colonists this was still a dangerous and unknown territory.

In the fall of 1587 Governor White returned to England for supplies, leaving behind the colonists, including his granddaughter, Virginia Dare, the first child born to English parents in the Western Hemisphere. A series of events in England delayed White's return to the Outer Banks for almost three years. When White returned to the Roanoke Island settlement in

August 1590, he found no trace of the colonists but only some of their scattered and ruined belongings. The only clue to the colonists' disappearance that White found was the word "Croatan" carved onto a tree. No one has been able to solve the mystery of what happened to the colonists and the meaning of "Croatan."

Some believe that Native Americans killed the settlers, as described on the mysterious stone tablets that were found in 1930. Others think that many of the settlers died from disease and that the remaining settlers joined Native American tribes. In 1998 an archaeological dig found evidence suggesting that some of the colonists might have joined the Croatans. A team digging at the ancient capital of Croatan chieftains on Hatteras Island found a sixteenth-century gold signet ring that probably belonged to one of the "Lost Colony."[3] Although many have theorized about the fate of the English colonists, what really happened to the Lost Colony remains a mystery to this day.

Perusing John White's 1585 map of the Outer Banks, which was the most accurate map drawn in the sixteenth century of any area of North America, one can ponder the Lost Colony's fate. Perhaps just as interesting is the fact that the map, which sketches the region from Cape Lookout to Chesapeake Bay, shows several topographical features that are changed today. On the Theodor de Bry engraving from 1590, which is what we see today of White's map, we see more inlets splitting the islands and Cape Kenrick (not named on the map) as the most easterly point of land on the map. Today all that remains of the cape is Wimble Shoals. In addition this marks the earliest occurrence of Hatrask (Hatteras), Wokokan (Ocracoke), Roanoac (Roanoke Island), and Croatoan on a map.

It was more than half a century after the Lost Colony's disappearance before the English attempted to settle the Outer Banks again. Permanent continuous settlement on the Outer Banks began in 1663 when Charles II issued the first land grant to Sir John Colleton. Shortly after that Captain John Whittle, Colleton's agent, established a plantation on what is today Colington Island. The managers planted crops such as corn and tobacco and raised livestock such as cattle and hogs. However, the plantation did not prosper in this difficult environment.

Although the harsh conditions on the Outer Banks were not ideal for plantation life, the conditions were ideal for another type of enterprise. For a short but colorful period from 1713 to 1718 pirates and smugglers such as Christopher Moody, Robert Deal, Charles Vane, "Calico Jack" Rackham, Anne Bonney, Mary Read, and Edward Teach (the most famous brigand) made the Outer Banks their home base for illegal activity. During this "Golden Age of Piracy" the pirates and smugglers, who terrorized ships on

"Arrival of the English," the 1590 White–de Bry map, is an accurate representation of the Outer Banks in the late sixteenth century, showing many topographical features that wind and sea have changed over the years. Courtesy of the University of North Carolina Library

the seas and colonists on the land, found the Outer Banks' treacherous shoals and dangerous inlets to be valuable allies in their nefarious escapades. Edward Teach, also known as "Blackbeard" because of his jet-black beard that he often braided and festooned with pieces of rope, wreaked the most havoc on ships. In battle Blackbeard would tie burning ribbons and cannon fuses to his beard so that he literally smoked while he fought.

The authorities did not tolerate the lawlessness for long but made a concerted and successful effort to capture the pirates. On November 22, 1718, British seamen under Lieutenant Robert Maynard killed the notorious Blackbeard, whose brief reign along the Outer Banks lasted less than a year. Blackbeard's demise ended the period of rampant piracy, although some activity continued until 1725. The important discovery of Blackbeard's sunken ship *Queen Anne's Revenge* in 1996 by the private group Intersal renewed interest in the pirate. Buried under sand in twenty feet of water

near Beaufort Inlet, the shipwreck has produced tens of thousands of artifacts such as ship parts and equipment, arms, scientific and navigational
instruments, personal effects, food-preparation items, cannons, and other
artifacts that provide important information about early-eighteenth-century
maritime culture. Various state agencies, educational institutions, and a
nonprofit group are studying and processing the conserved artifacts that
the North Carolina Maritime Museum will house.[4]

Even after the authorities quelled the pirate scourge, Bankers (as inhabitants were known) were few in number, concentrated in only a few towns,
and relatively isolated. By 1750 only one thousand people lived on the Outer
Banks, where survival was challenging. Vegetation was sparse; extreme
storms were always a threat; and no bridges connected the islands to each
other or to the mainland. Although Bankers found employment in shipbuilding, fishing, raising stock, and scavenging occasional shipwrecks,
there was no major industry to provide the number of jobs necessary for a
larger population.

The first significant industry on the Outer Banks—lightering—developed in the late eighteenth century. Lightering, a unique form of maritime
traffic, provided the bulk of the jobs for law-abiding Bankers, principally
around Ocracoke Inlet. Large trade ships arriving from Europe were unable to travel through the shallow Outer Banks inlets with their heavy
loads and would have their loads shifted to smaller boats at Ocracoke
Inlet. Once the large ships were lightered, as the process was known, the
smaller boats could travel through the inlets to the mainland. The lightering industry created jobs for pilots (who navigated the treacherous inlets)
and dockworkers (who loaded and unloaded the cargoes). By 1859 one
thousand people (one-third of the Outer Banks population) lived on either
side of Ocracoke Inlet. Most of the population depended directly or indi-
rectly on the lightering industry.

Government-funded projects provided some modest employment opportunities in the last decades of the nineteenth century. Following the
Civil War, the federal government built three lighthouses (Hatteras, Bodie
Island, and Currituck) and seven lifesaving stations that needed to be
staffed. Such projects provided employment opportunities and foreshad-
owed important governmental projects in the 1930s that would lead to a
more stable and tourism-based Outer Banks economy.

Tourism, the principal industry on the Outer Banks today, began as
early as the 1750s, when people traveled from the mainland to Ocracoke
and Portsmouth to enjoy the summer months at the shore. Mainland residents believed that visiting the Outer Banks was good for one's health.
Because many mainlanders died each summer from malaria (caused by

the mosquito-infested swamps), there was some truth to the belief. Summer visitors arrived at the shore initially by schooners, later by steamboats, and still later by automobiles after roads and bridges were built. Nags Head, the first important seashore resort on the Outer Banks, had become a popular seasonal vacation area by the 1830s.

Growth in tourism along the Outer Banks coincided with a period of increasing coastal use along the Atlantic seaboard. Between the 1840s and 1870s seaside resorts flourished along the Atlantic coastline, especially in the Northeast. Many wealthy New Yorkers built summer "cottages" and "villas" in Newport, Rhode Island, for example. During the 1860s and 1870s seaside resorts flourished from Cape May, New Jersey, to Bar Harbor, Maine.[5]

Although tourists were visiting the Outer Banks in the mid–eighteenth century, the oceanfront there was almost completely undeveloped well into the nineteenth century. In 1838 when entrepreneurs built the first Nags Head hotel complete with a grand ballroom, they did not build the two-hundred-guest building along the ocean but rather facing Albemarle Sound.[6] Until the mid–nineteenth century property owners did not build many primary, or even secondary, residences on the barrier islands and certainly not on the oceanfront. With so little demand for water-front property, land prices were extremely low. In the early 1830s Francis Nixon, a planter from Perquimans County, paid fifty cents per acre (equal to about ten dollars in 2009 dollars) for two hundred acres along the sound side in the Nags Head area.[7] Nixon and his friends, who soon followed, built the first summer cottages in the area.

It was not until 1866 that the first cottages were build along the shore by W. G. Pool. Dr. Pool, from Elizabeth City, North Carolina, paid members of the Midgett family sixty cents per acre (equal to about nine dollars in 2008 dollars)[8] for fifty acres bordering the ocean at Nags Head.[9] To entice others to join him, Pool offered the land to friends at prices that were less than he paid. The sea-loving troupe, knowing the changeability of the shoreline, adapted their lifestyle to the local environment. The families' thirteen "mobile" cottages were built only on foundations of pilings and without chimneys or utility connections. The homes were easily moved at the owners' whim or when shore-line erosion forced retreat. For example, the Outlaw family moved their house (which remains today) five times. In addition, since early owners built modest homes and used available materials, monetary loss owing to damage from storms was minimal. Because land was inexpensive and plentiful, owners had no reason to build barriers such as seawalls to protect their properties; they simply moved the homes farther back when necessary.

One of the mid-nineteenth-century beach houses that
became known as the "Unpainted Aristocracy"

In later years the cottages became known as the "Unpainted Aristocracy"
because of their modest but stately presence. Today, more than 130 years
after the homes were built, nine of the original thirteen cottages still stand
despite being buffeted by countless storms. While many homes built in
recent years along the Outer Banks have long since departed, those nine
remain partially because they have been mobile. The cottages have other
specific features that were built for nineteenth-century conditions. When
the Unpainted Aristocracy cottages were built, livestock freely roamed the
Outer Banks. During the hot summer days the wandering livestock, along
with their fleas, ticks, and flies, would search out the shade underneath
the houses. Bankers built latticework screens around the pilings to keep
the livestock from underneath the houses and the insect pests from invad-
ing the homes. Although the livestock no longer roam, the latticework,
which now provides only a decorative value, remains. One change, however, is that there is no longer any property nearby to which the owners
can move; one day the limited mobility will likely prove the undoing of the
remaining Unpainted Aristocracy.

Altering the Outer Banks

Humankind shaped the Outer Banks environment just as the sand and
sea shaped the people and environment. Humankind has altered the

environment there through two principal agents: the introduction of non-native species and technology.

Europeans introduced nonnative livestock such as cattle, sheep, and horses to the barrier islands shortly after permanent settlement in the late 1600s. By 1776 one observer commented that "all the sea banks [are] covered with cattle, sheep, and hogs, the few inhabitants living on the banks are chiefly persons whose estates consist in livestock."[10] The livestock freely roamed the islands, denuding the already sparse island vegetation. On a barrier island already susceptible to erosion, removing vegetation can lead to more shore-line erosion and exacerbate storm damage.

The alterations created by technology have caused the greatest environmental change on the Outer Banks. The principal technology that Native Americans would have used to alter the Outer Banks environment was fire, although it is unlikely that this had any lasting or wide-ranging impact on the environment. European settlement introduced much greater change. During the first two and one-half centuries of settlement, deforestation created the greatest impact on the Outer Banks environment, although humans plowed land, drained marshes, and stabilized inlets as well. Shipbuilding and lumbering, successful industries in the early 1800s, created the demand for live oak, pine, and cedar that depleted much of the forests. Boat builders cut large quantities of live oak (especially near Hatteras) that was used to build Yankee clippers before the Civil War. Spears reports that a sand wave moved across Cape Hatteras in the 1890s after Bankers cut large sections of forest on the shoreline.[11]

The effect that overgrazing and logging can have on barrier islands is evident on Shackleford Banks. In the nineteenth century the whaling community of Diamond City developed on Shackleford Island. The six hundred inhabitants of Diamond City cut many trees for firewood and boat construction and allowed livestock to overgraze the dunes. The denuded landscape became more susceptible to erosion and storm damage. The great August 1899 hurricane, which is often referred to as San Ciriaco, washed the unprotected dunes landward; over time the windblown dunes covered the remaining trees. Within three years of the hurricane, residents, who recognized that the island now provided less protection, moved three miles across the sound to Harker's Island or to other, mainland locations. Many floated their homes across the water on barges and repositioned them on new foundations. On Shackleford, which is returning to its natural state, a solitary cemetery is the only remaining indication that people once lived there. Recently as the dunes have shifted, formerly buried trees have emerged as evidence of the earlier dune migration. The tree stumps protruding from the sand on the seaward side of the island are the remnants of a maritime forest that once covered Shackleford Banks. Some mature maritime forest remains on the northern end of the island.[12]

Although Bankers began to effect changes to the islands in the late 1600s and continued through the eighteenth and nineteenth centuries, they did not create large-scale alterations until the twentieth century. In the early decades of the twentieth century conditions were bleak along the Outer Banks, which remained isolated and undeveloped. Wildfowl had been over-hunted, few ships wrecked along the coast, and no ships were being built. Additionally erosion was threatening many areas.[13] The only industry in which some Bankers could find employment was commercial fishing, which generated a meager income. However, activities begun in the 1920s would dramatically alter the Outer Banks and create the foundation for future development.

Businessmen who owned property on the Outer Banks recognized that roads and bridges would make the area more accessible to tourists and increase the land value. In 1924 land speculators from New Jersey encouraged Wash F. Baum, the mayor of Manteo, to begin infrastructure construction. Planners raised private as well as public funds to build the roads and bridges. The first bridge and causeway, financed by a Dare County bond project, was built from Manteo to Nags Head in 1927. In 1930 a group of Elizabeth City businessmen built the Wright Brothers Memorial Bridge across Currituck Sound with private funds.[14] Each bridge charged a toll of one dollar. The first paved roads on the Outer Banks soon followed, including the state highway through Kitty Hawk and Nags Head, which was completed in 1931. Before the paved roads, residents told visitors to the Outer Banks to take old 101 to get to their location; what the Bankers meant was to choose one of the 101 tracks in the sand. In 1937 the government built a bridge between the mainland and Roanoke Island.

However, officials needed a program to control shore-line erosion and keep roads free from drifting sand and ocean overwash before they could make any permanent improvements. A series of articles, beginning with one in the July 21, 1933, edition of the *Elizabeth City Independent,* proposed an ambitious project that included building new dunes and then stabilizing the dunes with plantings.[15]

Even if the engineering project could be accomplished, one obstacle would remain. In the 1930s horses, cattle, sheep, and hogs were permitted to roam freely on the Outer Banks and feed on the vegetation. To allow the new plantings to take hold, planners needed to stop livestock from eating the new growth before it had a chance to take hold. The solution required action from the state government. The North Carolina General Assembly passed the Livestock Act of 1934, which stopped open grazing on Ocracoke,

Hatteras, and Nags Head, although open grazing was still permitted on the Lower Banks—Portsmouth, Core Banks, Cape Lookout, and Shackleford Banks—until much later.[16]

The dune-stabilization project, coordinated by the National Park Service in collaboration with the CCC, began to roll. The goal of the project, which was directed by two engineers, A. C. Stratton and James R. Holloway, was to eliminate the flow of ocean water that would wash over the Outer Banks during the frequent storms. By the spring of 1934 the agencies had established six camps for more than fifteen hundred transient workers: three camps on the north tip of Roanoke Island and one each near Rodanthe, Frisco, and Ocracoke.[17] The project required extensive research and planning because so little was known about sand fixation. Researchers studied weather patterns for previous decades and created weather observation posts to study current weather patterns. Technicians researched fence construction in a specially created sand laboratory to determine the design that would trap sand and build dunes most effectively. After examining various types of sand fence construction, from wood slats to jute bagging, engineers discovered that the height and width of the fence determined the success. The most successful sand fence was an ordinary brush panel eight feet long and three feet wide that was between eight and twenty-five feet high; higher fences were built where erosion was most severe. Workers constructed the panels fifty miles inland where brush was available and then transported the panels to the shoreline.

Between 1936 and 1940 workers with the CCC and the Works Project Administration (WPA) erected a zigzag line of slatted fencing along 125 miles of beaches, including those on Hatteras, Pea, and Bodie islands. Once set in place, a fence would require about a year to trap enough sand to create foredunes that were 15 to 20 feet high and 150 feet wide, dunes that were large enough to block ocean overwash.[18]

However, the dunes would not remain in place for long without vegetation to anchor the sand. Planners set up experimental nurseries to determine which grasses, shrubs, and seedlings would stabilize the dunes most effectively. It was determined that grasses such as cordgrass, sea oats, American beach grass, and wire grass, which propagate through creeping stems that grow underground and anchor in loose sand, were most effective. CCC workers completed the stabilization project, which cost $3 million, by planting 142 million square feet of grasses and 2.5 million seedlings and shrubs to stabilize the beach sand.[19]

With the impressive bank of dunes in place, establishing a park would complete the project. Although the Cape Hatteras National Seashore was originally proposed in 1933, Congress did not authorize it until July 13,

Workers with the Civilian Conservation Corps (CCC) built sand fences in the 1930s as part of an ambitious plan to create dunes that would control shore-line erosion. Courtesy of the National Park Service, Cape Hatteras National Seashore

1937. World War II interrupted work on the park, and Nazi submarines trolling for ships off the coast forced blackouts in beach areas. Near the end of the war other interests almost halted the national seashore before it got any further. Oil companies began buying up mineral rights to drill offshore, and a small building boom ensued. The oil companies, along with real-estate developers, fought the proposed national park because of concerns that the park would halt drilling. In March 1945 the North Carolina legislature passed a bill that prohibited additional donations of land to the national seashore. However, the oil boom never occurred; the oil companies drilled their wells but abandoned their leases and the Outer Banks. Then in 1952, when the state of North Carolina matched a $618,000 gift from the Old Dominion Foundation and Avalon Foundation, the park became a reality.[20] The national seashore was established the following year, almost twenty years after it was first proposed.

Cape Hatteras National Seashore, the nation's first national seashore, protects seventy miles of shoreline stretching across three islands—Bodie, Hatteras, and Ocracoke—from Whalebone Junction, which is just south of Nags Head, to Ocracoke Inlet. Eight villages exist within the park boundaries and villagers' properties remain privately owned. Highlights for visitors include Coquina Beach, the Pea Island National Wildlife Refuge, and

Remnants of the *Laura Barnes,* which wrecked on Coquina Beach in 1921, are located at Cape Hatteras National Seashore. The shifting sands on this beach bury more and more of the schooner, which lies behind dunes constructed in the 1930s.

the Cape Hatteras and Bodie Island lighthouses, which the federal government built in 1870 and 1872 respectively.

Of interest is the fact that businessmen concerned with profit, not environmental protection, created the Cape Hatteras National Seashore. This motivation is similar to the one that led to the formation of Yellowstone National Park, which Congress established in 1872 as the United States' first national park.[21] In the late nineteenth century management of the Northern Pacific Railroad, which had a monopoly on transportation to the region, realized that the uniqueness of Yellowstone could draw large numbers of tourists to the area. The railroad management monopolized the park facilities, which in effect gave the company ownership of the park until automobiles were allowed to enter in 1915. On the Outer Banks, although no single owner was able to capture all of the rents produced by the tourists who would flock to the national park, local businessmen would jointly benefit from tourism dollars.

Following the establishment of Cape Hatteras National Seashore, several more projects linked the islands together. In the early 1950s the government built Highway 12, which connects Nags Head and Ocracoke, and in 1957 state-owned ferries began operation across Hatteras Inlet and between the mainland and Ocracoke. In 1963 the state government constructed the three-mile-long Herbert C. Bonner Bridge, which connected Bodie Island and Hatteras Island.[22] In 1966 Congress created Cape Lookout National Seashore, which extends another fifty-eight miles across Portsmouth Island, Core Banks, and Shackleford Banks; the southernmost islands are the most natural and unaltered sections of the Outer Banks.

Although the early history of the Outer Banks is interesting and the events of the early twentieth century have been instrumental to the area's development, important development started in the last half of the twentieth century. The single most important factor that has contributed to the Outer Banks economy of today is the 1930s erosion-control project—a project that planners hoped would mimic natural dunes and protect coastal areas. The dune-stabilization project, which created an effective barrier to ocean overwash, protected infrastructure and created a sense of security that encouraged development. The projects begun in the 1920s transformed the struggling Outer Banks economy—which depended on commercial fishing, maritime traffic, and the U.S. Coast Guard—into an economy that thrives on tourism.

Although planners hoped that the ambitious dune-stabilization project would halt island erosion and promote economic development, no one would have been able to predict how the Outer Banks would change over the remaining decades of the twentieth century. The dune-stabilization project, the construction of roads and bridges, the elimination of open stock range, and the establishment of the national park made the transformation possible. Federally sponsored projects such as the Wright Brothers National Monument and the reconstruction of Fort Raleigh on Roanoke Island, completed in 1932 and 1941 respectively, also became important tourist attractions. Other features make the Outer Banks a location that is desirable to so many. Kill Devil Hills, for example, was rated as the sixth-best beach for surfing in the United States, the highest ranking of any East Coast beach.[23]

As the last half of the twentieth century began, the Outer Banks was stabilized and primed for the development that transformed the isolated group of small villages into a thriving tourist community. Rapid growth and dramatic changes to the land have accompanied the transformation. Between 1970 and 2000, for example, the population in Currituck and Dare counties more than tripled, increasing from 13,971 to 48,157. Seasonal populations swell the area by an additional 200,000.

The rapid increase in the number of people on the Outer Banks has created many changes for communities. Larger houses with many more amenities have sprouted up along the shoreline. In Nags Head the average house

The Wright Brothers Monument, erected at the site of their first flight, is one of many Outer Banks tourist attractions created by the government.

At the northern end of Corolla (*below*) an ocean-to-sound fence prevents the resident herd of wild horses from roaming south. Until 1934 livestock ranged freely throughout the Outer Banks.

increased from fourteen hundred square feet and 3.3 bedrooms to twenty-five hundred square feet and 5 or more bedrooms from 1986 to 2000. Homes as large as five thousand square feet are not uncommon, and rental homes as large as ten thousand square feet with 16 bedrooms have been built.[24] Large ocean-front homes that provide seasonal rentals have replaced the smaller single-family cottages that were once a popular form of accommodation for visitors. The new, multistory, high-occupancy rentals are basically small motels accommodating several families.

Developers even build communities in places where paved roads do not exist. Four-wheel-drive vehicles travel along the unpaved beach for the seventeen miles between Corolla and the Virginia border to a recent housing development. Curiously amid the development is a poignant reminder of the days when livestock roamed freely and Bankers held "Pony Penning" on the Fourth of July.[25] Today a herd of about one hundred Outer Banks wild horses wanders fifteen thousand acres of public and private land beyond the end of Highway 12. Currituck County designated the area, which includes the Currituck National Wildlife Refuge, the North Carolina Estuarine Research Reserve, and land owned by the Nature Conservancy, as a Wild Horse Sanctuary in 1989.

Some evidence indicates that the horses are descended from Spanish mustangs that first arrived on the Outer Banks some four hundred years ago when Spanish galleons wrecked on the treacherous shores. The current management plan limits the herd to 60 horses, although a recent study recommends that an ideal number would be 110 to allow the herd's survival. However, the U.S. Fish and Wildlife Service is concerned that more than 60 horses grazing the area will harm migratory birds and other species. This is one more illustration of the conflicts that develop when limited resources restrict choices.

The development of the tourism industry has caused increased employment opportunities and economic growth in recent decades and has created dramatic changes along the Outer Banks. Dare County is the most tourism-dependent county in North Carolina.[26] Land conversion is occurring at a faster rate than population growth as open spaces are developed. Along with the housing development, commercial businesses and shopping malls have multiplied. A close-knit community with a shared history has become a community of fenced-in yards, shopping malls, and traffic lights.

On John White's 1585 Outer Banks map we see the islands' topography as the first European explorers viewed it. The map is quite accurate—especially considering that White would not have been able to survey the entire coastline. Today, although barrier-island migration has moved the Outer Banks about a mile west of the location recorded on White's map (more than four centuries earlier), the general shape of the area is the same. One noticeable change is that Cape Kendrick has been washed away; Wimble Shoals is all that remains of the cape. Although the topography is little changed, twentieth-century development has changed the Outer Banks in other ways that would convince White's party that they were in a completely foreign place. Today as you drive along Highway 12 between Rodanthe and Nags Head, a solid line of dunes blocks your view of the ocean. Although the dunes would be familiar to the early explorers, the development that was encouraged by the idea of "stabilizing" the islands would not be. The dunes constructed during the 1930s project, which have survived into the twenty-first century, provide infrastructure and buildings some protection from the vagaries of such a precarious location. This project has had a greater impact on the Outer Banks than any other alteration by humans.

The economic development that followed the 1930s project has changed the character of the islands. Islands can be exotic, mysterious, and secluded places that evoke images from adventure stories such as *Robinson Crusoe, Treasure Island,* and the *Island of Dr. Moreau.* The bridges that now connect the Outer Banks to the mainland and usher over crowds of tourists change the islands' special characteristics. Now once-isolated communities are annexed by the mainland; a sense of independence that islands enjoy is diminished (although when a hurricane is approaching or when one needs urgent medical attention, a bridge is welcome). Today the Outer Banks has a vibrant economy that depends on the government—an active tourist economy anchored by the national seashore. Although some may express dissatisfaction with the current Outer Banks development, it seems the die is cast. However, as will be discussed later, changing conditions for the Outer Banks and other coastal communities will require adaptations if the communities are to be sustainable.

Four

Understanding the "Sea of Troubles" Facing Coastal Communities

What is common to the greatest number gets the least amount of care.

Aristotle

Economic growth and development have changed the Outer Banks rapidly in recent decades. Unfortunately sometimes the development damages the island environment. In order to understand why we spoil coastal areas that we value so much, we must understand how incentives affect decision makers. For example, although few livestock can be found anywhere on the Outer Banks and only a limited number of horses are allowed to roam freely in limited areas, Outer Bankers allowed livestock to roam without restriction well into the twentieth century and long after other parts of the country had fenced them in. Understanding the events that led to fenced-in livestock in most of the United States by the end of the nineteenth century will provide a model that can help explain decisions that shape the Outer Banks today. The place to begin the story is out west, where two centuries ago the cowboys who herded cattle on the open plains provided the inspiration for many tall tales.

Incentives Matter

In America in the first half of the nineteenth century, ranchers allowed livestock (principally sheep, cattle, and horses) to roam freely over the great plains of the Southwest, where the law of the open range ruled. With land so plentiful, ranchers had no need to fence in the livestock that were allowed to wander the plains. If a cowboy found a valley already occupied by someone's herd, he simply moseyed the herd onto the next open range. Besides, the cost of fencing was prohibitive in the West, unlike in the East, where rocks and trees were more plentiful. We can imagine that "seldom was heard a discouraging word" on the wide expanse of tall-grass prairies that supported millions of bison for generations of Native Americans.

By the 1860s and 1870s, however, times were changing. Following the Civil War beef prices shot up, and in response ranchers expanded their

Cattle and other livestock were allowed to roam the Outer Banks without restriction long after other areas of the United States required ranchers to fence in livestock. In this 1930s photograph, cattle graze on Portsmouth Island. Photograph by Aycock Brown; courtesy of the Outer Banks History Center, Manteo, North Carolina

herds. As pasturelands became scarcer and thus more valuable, ranchers began to see the advantage of restricting access to the land. With growing demand for grazing land, ranchers began to realize that even the great expanse of the Wild West had limits. In addition fencing in one's cattle would help protect one's investment; a fenced-in cow would be less likely to wander off or be stolen by rustlers. Cowmen began forming stock growers' associations that passed laws to limit entry onto formerly common-owned land. However, ranchers still faced the prohibitive expense of fencing wide expanses of land. As is often the case, the potential to make a profit is the father of invention.

Although good-quality smooth wire was readily available before 1870, it was not a dependable deterrent to livestock passage. What ranchers needed was wire that would stop cattle from roaming and discourage trespassers and rustlers. Out of Illinois came the solution—barbed wire. Joseph Glidden of Dekalb, Illinois, is credited with inventing barbed wire in 1873, although the battle among inventors was a little like an Old West gunfight. Jacob Haish, who submitted barbed-wire patents at about the same time as Glidden, claimed to be the first. When the dust had cleared, the U.S.

Supreme Court declared Glidden the owner of the first barbed-wire patent. Ingenious competitors thought of numerous variations on the theme and created an additional 529 barbed-wire patents that satiated western ranchers' desires.

Although barbed wire provided the means to enclose the plains in a cost-effective way, many independent-minded westerners, armed with six-shooters and wire cutters, bitterly fought the enclosure movement. The often violent "fence cutter wars" led to many deaths and heavy financial costs before the resistance was broken by large landowners who began fencing their boundaries. The owners of the Frying Pan ranch, Henry Sanborn and Joseph Glidden (two of the Illinois barbed-wire inventors), strung 150 miles of barbed-wire fencing at a price of more than thirty-nine thousand dollars to contain fifteen hundred head of cattle. Other large Texas Panhandle ranchers, such as those at the XIT and the JA ranches, strung barbed wire across many more miles of land, and the days of free-range grazing were over.

Changing incentives motivated ranchers to end the open range. Higher livestock values that increased the demand for land and affordable fencing that allowed the enclosure of the wide prairies at a reasonable cost caused the evolution of property rights from open grazing to private ownership and restrictions on access.[1] A similar evolution of livestock grazing rights occurred in the southeastern states. In the Southeast in colonial times farmers were required to build fences around their crops in order to keep free-ranging livestock out. Virginia passed one of the earliest "fence-out" laws in 1632; the law required all cultivators to build fences around their crops or suffer the consequences of roaming livestock. Colonists in most areas of the Southeast considered unfenced land to be open pasture.[2]

Laws required livestock enclosure in some intensely cultivated and more populous areas in the South well before the Civil War. For example, in 1785 South Carolina prohibited hogs from roaming in two lowcountry counties, and Virginia and North Carolina abolished the open range in large sections of those states by the late 1850s. After the Civil War livestock enclosure laws became common; Georgia began limiting open-range grazing in 1872, and other states followed soon after. By 1890 there were few places in the country where livestock could roam freely. One of the exceptions was the Outer Banks.

As early as the 1660s, when the first stable settlements began on the Outer Banks, it was common to see cattle and other livestock roaming the islands and feeding on verdant inland marsh grass and other island grasses. The more modest island expanses allowed far fewer livestock than the open plains did. However, unlike other areas of the country, the Outer

Banks permitted open grazing on all the islands until 1934 and until 1966 on some islands. Conditions specific to the Outer Banks explain the delay on open-grazing restrictions.

Enclosure was unnecessary to protect a Banker's investment. Livestock owners did not worry about losing wandering livestock because before long the livestock would run up against a natural boundary of water. Cattle rustlers would have a hard time moving stolen cattle across the sounds. In addition no large predators such as wolves or fast-moving vehicles such as trains threatened the livestock. Furthermore owners did not have to worry about wandering livestock damaging farmers' crops because only limited subsistence farming was practiced on the sandy soil found on the Outer Banks. Therefore the invention of barbed wire, which was never widely used on the Outer Banks, made little impact on grazing decisions.

Because not many people lived on the Outer Banks until the final decades of the twentieth century, the demand for land was modest. Bankers could use the land for less productive enterprises such as grazing. The few people who made homes on the Outer Banks kept relatively small numbers of livestock because the land could not support large herds. Consequently the demand for grazing land was low. Essentially on the Outer Banks the benefits of open grazing were greater than the costs. Open grazing allowed Bankers to feed their livestock at no cost to the individual and only nominal costs to the commons.

However, the circumstances changed in the 1930s, when planners decided to create a national park. Planners recognized that livestock would have to be restricted from grazing the dunes in order to protect the new seedlings that were to be planted to solidify the dunes. When planners began the dune-building project, the state legislature passed the Livestock Act of 1934, which stopped open grazing on Ocracoke, Hatteras, and Nags Head, the areas where the dunes would be built.[3]

Without access to the island commons, livestock production quickly declined because the cost to feed the livestock was prohibitive. The government closed the last remaining open grazing area in 1966, when Shackleford Banks became part of Cape Lookout National Seashore. After open grazing was halted, only a few Bankers continued ranching on private land for a short time. At Corolla, Ernie Bowden was able to maintain a herd of almost one hundred cattle and several buffalo until 1989 by leasing inexpensive marshland from hunting clubs.

Today livestock grazing is no longer practiced anywhere on the Outer Banks because land is more valuable when used for other purposes. Once the land became more valuable as a national park, the benefits of controlling access to the commons outweighed the benefits of open grazing, and

Bankers realized that restricting wandering livestock would improve the economy.

The decision to stop open grazing was integral to the development of the Outer Banks. However, the moral of the story has a much broader application and helps explain why we do not do a better job of protecting the environment so important to our quality of life. After all, we depend on a healthy environment for our life support system, the resources to produce the goods we need, and the amenities that enrich our lives. Indeed the tourists so important to the local economy would not crowd the Outer Banks if they found polluted waters and eroded beaches. Why then do we often treat valuable resources so poorly? The answer lies in the problem known as the "tragedy of the commons."

Often humans inadvertently damage resources, such as beaches and waterways, that many share but no one owns. For example, runoff from roadways, farms, parking lots, and residential development damages estuaries. The problem is that to the individual, the benefit (not paying to control the runoff) is greater than the cost of using the common-owned resource. However, to society the cost of the runoff is greater than the benefit as the shared estuary becomes polluted. The failure to protect common-owned resources is known as the "tragedy of the commons."[4] The adage by Aristotle at the beginning of this chapter explains why the "tragedy" occurs.

The "tragedy" would have occurred on the stabilized dunes in the 1930s if the legislature had not passed the Livestock Act. When access to grazing the dunes was open to all, no individual had an incentive to stop his or her livestock from grazing there. Indeed, even if one chose to stop grazing livestock on the dunes, some other Bankers' cattle would have eaten the grass seedlings, and the dunes would have been destabilized. When the benefits of limiting access to the commons became greater than the costs of limiting access, society acted to protect the dunes vegetation.

When access to a resource is not limited and demand for the resource is high, we tend to misuse it. For resources such as fisheries and waterways, this is the case. As coastal areas become more crowded, the problems become more difficult to solve; this calls into question some government policies that subsidize the growth. Hurricanes and shore-line erosion create problems for coastal communities that challenge policy makers as well.

Overusing the Fishery Commons

Ocean fisheries, which are an important source of protein for the world, provide an excellent illustration of the "tragedy of the commons," unfortunately. This was not always the case. During a 1584 expedition on the Outer

Banks, Captain Barlowe reported that a Native American filled his canoe "as deep as it could swimme" with "bountiful" fish from the sound. A John White painting shows Native Americans catching "bountiful" fish, including sturgeon and hammerhead sharks, which are now rarely seen in the sounds.

Historically marine fishing resources were thought to be limitless. As recently as the 1960s, fishery harvests around the world were increasing, and the Stratton Commission released an important report in 1969 that predicted that landings would expand worldwide by eight to ten times. Given the optimistic projections and programs such as the Capital Construction Fund and Fishing Vessel Obligation Guarantee Program, which provided incentives for U.S. fishers, the domestic fishing industry expanded its capacity to catch fish rapidly.[5] In 1976 Congress approved the Magnuson-Stevens Fishery Conservation and Management Act (MSFA) to manage and assert U.S. control over fishery resources within two hundred nautical miles of the coast. Unfortunately the expectations of bounty were wrong, and the act has performed ineffectively.

In recent decades many ocean fisheries, including those along the Outer Banks, have been overfished. It now appears that fish landings were already at their peak in the late 1960s. Within the next two decades the North Atlantic cod fishery drastically declined, and by the 1990s Canada completely shut down its cod fishery. In 1996 the Sustainable Fisheries Act, which revised the MSFA, required actions to eliminate overfishing, minimize bycatch, and protect fishery habitats. Unfortunately worldwide thirteen of the seventeen major ocean fisheries are being overexploited. Recent studies have emphasized the necessity to curb overfishing.[6] As one study concluded, "the last thirty years have witnessed overexploitation of many fish stocks, degradation of habitats, and negative consequences for too many ecosystems and fishing communities. To ensure the long-term sustainability of U.S. fisheries, maximize social and economic benefits, and reinforce the principle that living marine resources are held in public trust for the benefit of all U.S. citizens, fishery management must be improved."[7]

Although not as bountiful as when the Barlowe expedition explored the area, the Outer Banks fisheries remain diverse and productive in many regards. In 2008 North Carolina commercial fishers caught more than seventy-one million pounds of fish, which sold for more than eighty-seven million dollars. Commercial fishers harvested sixty-eight types of finfish and fifteen species of shellfish. Recreational fishers, who have increased landings in recent decades, harvested sixteen million pounds in 2008; they caught thirty-five of the species of fish that commercial fishers caught.[8] However, the North Carolina Division of Marine Fisheries, which assesses the stock of the state's fisheries annually, has reported that eight species are overfished. The overfished species are black sea bass, striped bass, southern flounder, river herring, spiny dogfish, Atlantic sturgeon, tautog, and weakfish. Of the other thirty-two fish stocks that are listed in a report, there is concern about eight other species, the conditions of six species are unknown, and eighteen are viable and recovering species.[9]

The friction between commercial and recreational fishers is an indication of the stressed ocean fisheries. With both groups of fishers vying for many of the same species of fish, such as red drum, spotted sea trout, and flounder, organizations have been instigating legislative solutions. House Bill 918, which was introduced in the 2009 North Carolina legislative session, would prohibit the sale and purchase of red drum and spotted sea trout and prohibit the use of nets to catch the fish. The argument made by the Coastal Fisheries Reform Group (an interest group for recreational fishers) and others is that allowing only recreational fishers to catch the fish would create greater economic benefits for the Outer Banks and North Carolina. Recreational fishers contribute much to the local economy by hiring fishing guides, eating in restaurants, and staying in hotels, for example.

Fishers who are overusing the ocean commons are not villains but are supplying what consumers are demanding. With increasing world demand for fish and open access, there simply are not enough fish in the sea any longer. When a single bluefin tuna can sell for eighty thousand dollars or more, it is no wonder that fishers are fishing this species to extinction. In addition, with improved technology such as radar, spotter planes, and bigger nets and lines, fishers are able to catch more fish at lower cost. Trawling nets large enough to swallow twelve jumbo jets in a single gulp, longlines stretching for seventy-five miles with thousands of hooks, and huge drift nets are some of the modern tools that contribute to overharvesting.

Although fisheries are not limitless, if managed in a sustainable way, fisheries could remain productive indefinitely. For example, if a fish population of twenty tons grew by a mass of one ton every year, fishers could harvest one ton every year and still have a fishery of twenty tons available annually. Although enhanced fish-catching capability contributes to overfishing, the principal problem is that demand for the resources has increased and no one controls access to the commons. There is virtually no incentive for fishers to practice conservation because any fish that an angler sets free can be caught and sold by someone else. Here we have the "tragedy of the commons." The fishers will lose as well because fish populations will be overharvested, and catches, as well as profits, will decline.

Human activities such as pollution and natural causes such as weather both affect a fishery, which is an interactive resource. Oyster harvests on

the Outer Banks, which were low in the 1990s, illustrate the interconnec-
tions. North Carolina oyster stocks, which peaked at 1.8 million bushels in
1902, were in a state of decline for most of the twentieth century. The Division of Marine Fisheries lists the current stock status for oysters as a "concern." Factors that have contributed to the reduction in oyster numbers
are disease, reduced water quality, and increased harvest pressure, although
the combined effect of these factors is not understood completely. In addition many fisheries depend on coastal habitat areas that are damaged by
activities such as filling in wetlands and installing jetties.

In recent years the increasing amount of coastal development and storm-
water runoff is correlated with the increasing closures to harvest of shell-
fishing waters. Water pollution is of particular concern to coastal areas such
as the Outer Banks because water is so prevalent. The principal polluters
of coastal waterways can be classified as point-source and non-point-source
polluters. Point-source polluters are generally firms and municipalities that
dump waste into a waterway. An example of a non-point-source polluter,
which is more difficult to control, is runoff from urban developments and
farms.

Crowding the Shore

The "tragedy of the commons" explains why we overfish the ocean, over-
develop communities, destroy habitats, and pollute air, water, and land.
However, the 1934 livestock law that stopped open grazing on the Outer
Banks illustrates that society can choose to control the overuse of the commons, especially when provided with the proper incentives. Unfortunately
protecting the commons becomes more difficult as more people crowd an
area and thus increase pressure on scarce resources. This is just what has
been happening in recent decades on the Outer Banks and in coastal communities in general.

Increasing numbers of people have been visiting and moving to coastal
areas such as the Outer Banks in recent decades. Although much of the
U.S. coastline remained thinly populated until after World War II, coastal
populations have increased rapidly. A National Oceanic and Atmospheric
Administration (NOAA) report on coastal population trends in the United
States shows that from 1980 to 2003 coastal population increased from 120
to 153 million people, an increase of 28 percent.[10] In addition projections
have suggested that another 11 million people would move to coastal counties by the year 2008, for another 7 percent increase. Coastal populations
have been growing by 12 to 13 million each decade, and by 2015 the number of people living in coastal areas is expected to increase to 165 million.
With more than half of the U.S. population crowded onto only 17 percent

of the land, this puts a large, and growing, number of people in a very small area of the country. If the projections are correct, population density will have increased from 187 to 327 persons per square mile from 1960 to 2015; this is more than three times the national average.[11]

While coastal populations are increasing in most areas, the southeastern coastline is experiencing a disproportionate amount of growth. Between 1960 and 2010 population near U.S. shorelines is expected to have increased by 60 percent but by 181 percent along the southeastern coast.[12] Coastal population density of the southeastern region increased from 142 to 224 persons per square mile between 1980 and 2003 and is expected to increase to 241 by 2008. The current southeast region population density is two and one-half times the population density of the nation, which is 98 persons per square mile. Outer Banks growth was slower than in many other coastal areas, even after the construction of bridges and roads there in the 1930s, because the Outer Banks was not near major population centers. However, in recent decades population on the Outer Banks has increased dramatically. Dare County's population increased by 328 percent from 1970 to 2000, and Currituck County's population increased by 161 percent for the same period.

Many factors have contributed to the increasing number of people frequenting coastal areas over the last half-century. The U.S. population became more mobile as transportation infrastructure improved, allowing travelers to get to the beach in less time. The interstate system was developed, airline travel expanded, and bridges were built to some of the islands during recent decades. As income rose, especially for the middle class, people traveled more and purchased second homes in coastal areas. Many senior citizens have retired with increased savings, which allows them to visit and move to coastal areas. In addition the maturation of the tourism industry has facilitated travel.

A period of rapid suburbanization began in the United States in the 1950s as the automobile and a developing interstate highway system allowed people to commute from greater distances to work. Throughout the last half of the twentieth century the trend of moving to the suburbs continued and expanded, with many people moving to the coast. Companies joined the flight to the suburbs and coastal areas, moving from cities blighted with crime and high costs to the friendlier suburbs. Firms that originally located in city centers to be near transportation nodes or next to rivers for energy are increasingly footloose today and are no longer tied to a particular location. In the twenty-first century, with information technology allowing more companies to move wherever they want, companies often choose to move to places that appeal to their workers, such as coastal areas. As a

result more businesses are moving from the suburbs to smaller communities, many of which are "gateway communities." Gateway communities are
near areas of great natural beauty such as a mountain range or the seashore. As workers, families, and companies become even more footloose,
owing in part to changing technology, even more are likely to locate near
coastal areas.

Other factors have encouraged population growth along the southeastern coast and the Outer Banks. A twentieth-century invention made the
southern coastline more appealing to many. In 1901 Willis Carrier invented
air conditioning, which became available in the 1930s and began to be
widely used after the 1950s. Air conditioning made southern summers more
bearable for those not comfortable with the high heat and humidity. In
addition the population growth in nearby areas such as Hampton, Virginia,
and Raleigh-Durham, North Carolina, created a large number of people
within driving distance of the Outer Banks. Lower property prices on the
Outer Banks as well, relative to other coastal areas, have increased the
demand for property there.

Government Encouraged Development

Until recent decades the threat of shore-line erosion and storm damage
made ocean shore-line property a poor investment value for most, especially on barrier islands where structures were likely to be damaged. When
early inhabitants of the Outer Banks built homes, they settled primarily on
the sound side or in the maritime forest to minimize the risk from storms
and beach erosion. The advantages were that the high dunes and forest
vegetation offered some protection from severe weather and that therefore
beach erosion posed no threat. If residents built near the oceanfront, as did
the owners of the Unpainted Aristocracy, they built modest, movable structures because they recognized the hazards of ocean-front living. The first
ocean-front homes (circa 1866), which were simple, functional, and mobile,
were built with salvaged materials from shipwrecks. If a storm destroyed
such a home, not much monetary value was lost. When erosion brought
the sea too close to home, owners simply moved back a little farther. However, things have changed. Today many more people are not only crowding
the shore but also building bigger houses, and in many cases these houses
are closer to the shore.

Why have building patterns changed so much? Although storms and erosion still threaten coastal areas, over the last several decades government
policies have reduced the risk of property damage that property owners
must bear. The government-funded dune-stabilization project that CCC and
WPA workers completed on the Outer Banks created a sense of security

Dunes created by the CCC and WPA construction project. The government-funded stabilization project encouraged the development of the Outer Banks. Courtesy of the National Park Service, Cape Hatteras National Seashore

that encouraged new development. In addition the stabilized dunes allowed the government to construct infrastructure such as roadways and the Bonner Bridge. Such government programs have encouraged the development of the Outer Banks.

Often government policies that are intended to solve problems create costly and undesirable outcomes. One example is the National Flood Insurance Program (NFIP), which was implemented in 1968. Although private insurance companies write flood insurance policies, the federal government (through the NFIP) determines the rates and pays for any damage costs not covered by insurance premiums. The federal government began the NFIP in order to save lives and reduce expensive government payments resulting from flood-related natural disasters. The NFIP provides subsidized flood insurance to flood-prone communities that agree to guide development away from the locations most likely to be flooded. In addition planners must institute building codes that make homes storm resistant. Unfortunately the NFIP is encouraging more, not less, development in dangerous locations.

Some twenty thousand communities participate in the NFIP, which insures $1.2 trillion worth of property through almost six million policies. The current maximum limit of coverage is $250,000 for residential property structure and $100,000 for contents, and $500,000 for nonresidential properties for both structure and contents. Since its inception in 1968, the NFIP has paid out $36.7 trillion in insurance payments; $770 million has been paid for damage to North Carolina properties.[13] Federal flood insurance covers only structural damage caused by flooding and does not cover wind damage or damage to land. New or reconstructed buildings in the floodplain must be elevated at or above the one-hundred-year flood level. For communities that undertake flood-plain mitigation activities beyond minimum requirements, the Community Rating System provides additional discounts on insurance premiums. Nags Head, for example, which has a class seven rating, receives an additional 15 percent discount.[14]

Unfortunately the NFIP encourages the very activity that the policy is meant to prevent. This is known as a "moral hazard"; that is, because a property owner receives inexpensive property insurance that protects against flooding, he or she will be more likely to build in a location that is likely to flood. Only after the passage of the NFIP did many home owners began building the large, expensive homes that crowd the shore today. Moreover many of the houses are built in the locations most likely to suffer property damage from severe storms. With subsidized insurance more home owners choose to build in hazardous areas because they do not bear the full costs of their lifestyles. One study estimates that over the last twenty years the NFIP has been responsible for a 15 percent development density in high-risk coastal areas.[15] Local planning, which was supposed to move development away from hazardous areas, has been ineffective because powerful interests such as the real-estate industry and property owners want to develop the most desirable (and often most hazardous) locations next to the ocean.

It is no accident that damage costs from hurricanes have multiplied since the implementation of the NFIP. Until Hurricane Diane in 1955 no storm had ever cost a billion dollars. Today, with so many million-dollar homes along the shore, multibillion-dollar storms are the rule. Although the government has scaled back the insurance subsidy in recent years, the costs to taxpayers are still substantial. The premiums paid by the insured would pay only about 38 percent of the full-risk premium needed to fund the long-term expectation for losses.[16] The subsidy is especially costly because home owners can rebuild their homes repeatedly at taxpayers' expense. Repetitive losses (that is, insured properties that have each sustained two or more flood losses of at least one thousand dollars in any ten-year

A house threatened by shore-line erosion. Government policies encourage property owners to construct housing in such high-hazard areas.

period) are a major cost of the NFIP. Between 1978 and 1995 U.S. taxpayers paid almost $2.6 billion for repetitive loss properties.[17] In Nags Head, for example, at least 116 properties are repetitive loss structures.[18]

A recent study has found that undervaluing erosion hazards, which NFIP insurance premiums do not adjust for, subsidizes home owners as well.[19] Over the next several decades an average of fifteen hundred homes and the land on which they are built will be lost to erosion each year. Although the NFIP does not cover all erosion damage, the program reimburses most erosion-related losses. However, flood insurance rates, which are based on flood risk alone, do not reflect erosion damage costs. To reflect erosion risk completely, insurance rates in the highest risk coastal areas would have to be, on average, twice today's rates.

State government policies provide insurance that encourages development in hazard-prone areas as well. In addition to flood insurance, property owners along the southeastern U.S. coast purchase insurance against damage from high winds. Home owners may be able to obtain privately underwritten policies to cover damage from wind, but some private insurance companies will no longer cover high-risk areas such as those on coasts or will provide insurance only at very high rates. In order to help coastal property owners, the North Carolina legislature in 1969 created an insurance pool known as the Beach Plan, which provides coverage from wind damage, specifically for property owners on the Outer Banks. The program was expanded in 1998 to eighteen coastal counties. Administered by the North Carolina Department of Insurance, the program insures 170,000 properties worth $72 billion. Unfortunately a major hurricane could inflict $3 billion of property damage, and the program has only $2.4 billion worth of assets.

In August 2009 North Carolina legislators revised the Beach Plan, which was seriously underfunded. The new plan raised property owners' rates to cover expected losses and reduced the risk of special assessments; it will also encourage more private competition. Coastal homeowners who purchase wind-pool insurance can get coverage for $750,000, half of the $1.5 million that was previously available. Those needing more coverage must go to private insurance markets. The policy change reduces the subsidy to the wealthiest property owners. Under the new plan, for example, the owner of a four-thousand-square-foot house on Emerald Isle will pay $15,700 annually, a 26 percent increase over the previous payment.[20]

State and federal governments lower the costs of living near shorelines further by paying a large portion of the cost of beach nourishment, which replenishes sand on eroded beaches. East Coast barrier islands, including the Outer Banks, receive more beach nourishment sand than any other region in the country. Between 1923 and 1996, 350 million cubic yards of sand were placed on East Coast beaches. A dramatic increase in nourishment began in the 1970s and escalated in the last two decades of the twentieth century. More than 50 percent of all nourishment was completed between 1980 and 1996, and almost 30 percent was completed between 1990 and 1996. The authors of a study conclude that a major reason for the recent increased nourishment activity is the increased availability of federal funding. The federal government paid about 65 percent of all nourishment costs, although state and local governments and private interests paid an increasing share of the costs.[21] Current federal government appropriations for beach nourishment total approximately $150 million per year.[22] The federal government pays 65 to 95 percent of beach nourishment costs for federally approved projects, although in recent years the federal government has been balking at funding for upkeep of beaches.

In order to ensure the wise use of taxpayer dollars, the U.S. Army Corps of Engineers (ACE) does a benefit-cost analysis of all projects, such as beach nourishment, that receive federal funding. However, the agency, which makes numerous assumptions in each analysis, could exaggerate the benefits and minimize the costs of projects in order to justify funding. A report by the U.S. Army inspector general found that the ACE was "institutionally biased" toward approving expensive projects, going so far as intentionally changing data to justify one large-scale project.[23] As a result nourishment projects that are not creating net benefits may be completed.

In addition federal programs provide poststorm assistance such as Federal Emergency Management Agency (FEMA) disaster relief, tax write-offs for disaster losses, replacement of infrastructure, and paying for cleanup costs, which lower the costs of coastal development even further. For example, one year after Hurricane Fran, which struck in 1996, the federal government had provided an estimated $10,500 in assistance per year-round resident for the three North Carolina barrier islands of Topsail, Wrightsville Beach, and Pleasure Island.[24]

Governmental subsidies encourage costly housing developments on the Outer Banks and other coastal areas by shielding property owners from the adverse financial consequences that can result from natural disasters. Not only do the subsidies encourage development in risky areas, but taxpayers from across the country are paying for the costs created by those who choose to build in coastal areas. Programs such as the NFIP encourage costly developments inland as well; farmers in midwestern states, for example, have received help with insurance coverage for flood-prone areas along rivers. Such subsidies are inefficient and inequitable whether coastal or inland property owners are the beneficiaries.

Government subsidies are not completely responsible for coastal development. One study has concluded that rising income levels and employment in nearby inland areas have increased the demand for recreation, which has created most of the growth in beach-front communities.[25] According to the authors of the study, public investment in beach nourishment has little or no effect on coastal development, although subsidized federal flood insurance appears to have contributed to coastal development.

Benefits and Costs of Economic Development

Some maintain that government subsidies that encourage coastal development are justified because they lead to economic growth. On the Outer Banks, where the tourism and construction industries provide much of the job base, coastal development has contributed a lot to the local economy. Economic development provides benefits such as jobs, income, and an expanded tax base that government can use for infrastructure improvements. Many residents, especially landowners and businesspeople who generally benefit the most from development, welcome the revenue and jobs generated by economic development.

Many believe that the tourism industry is more desirable than many other types of industries. Generally tourism creates less damage to the environment and less loss of aesthetics than do many other industries, such as manufacturing. Tourism may offer benefits besides monetary ones. As communities recognize that natural areas, such as beaches, draw tourists, broader support for environmental protection may result.

However, economic development, including the tourism industry, can be costly. Although the influx of residents and tourists may create a robust economy, the environment may suffer. Increasing demand for land conversion from open space to residential and commercial uses creates the familiar "sprawl" problems. Development often damages sensitive ecosystems such as wetlands, which provide wildlife habitat, mitigate flooding, and purify water. Development may increase non-point-source water pollution such as runoff from roads and parking lots. The polluted waterways, which lead to closings of shell-fishing areas and beaches, create additional costs. Other negative impacts from development include increased traffic, visual pollution, and air pollution.

An increase in population will increase requests for beach nourishment to protect property. Beach nourishment, which is undertaken to slow shoreline erosion that threatens developed areas, may damage beach and nearshore habitats. For example, nourishment sand can cover fish habitat, reefs, and food sources, such as crabs and clams, on which birds depend. The dredged sand may be contaminated with toxic substances that could be released onto the nourished beaches. In addition if the new sand is too compact, sea turtles may not be able to nest.

Economic development can create land-use changes that alter the character of the community. Open spaces are lost, and the community becomes overcrowded. In addition new growth requires investment in roads, sewage, and other infrastructure. The costs for the new infrastructure, such as water and sewer facilities, may outweigh the benefits generated by the economic growth. Many of the jobs created by growth, especially in the service-oriented tourism industry, may be low paying and filled by new workers moving into the community rather than local residents.

With growing numbers of people looking for increasingly scarce coastal property, land prices increase—a lot! In 1934 an acre of land near Nags Head sold for about $60, which would be the equivalent of $961 in 2009 dollars.[26] Ocean-front lots that in 1993 sold for $250,000 went for three to four times that in 2003.[27] In 2005 the average selling price for an Outer Banks home was $544,893, up a staggering 121 percent from 2000.[28] High property taxes that accompany escalating land values may force longtime residents to sell and move elsewhere. The cohesiveness and character of a community will change. (The slow housing market in recent years did cause average prices to decline on the Outer Banks, just as in most housing markets across the country. The average Outer Banks house sold for $417,507 in 2008, for example, down 10.5 percent from the previous year.)

Offshore Oil Drilling

Offshore oil drilling can create economic benefits such as tax revenues, jobs, and income but also economic costs. No oil company has pumped oil from along the Outer Banks coast, but several companies have made plans to exploit the area. In the 1940s several companies drilled exploratory off-shore wells. The oil companies, together with some residents who believed that oil production would be good for the local economy, tried to stop the establishment of the Outer Banks as a national seashore. Oil interests were concerned that the group intent on creating the designation would try to stop the companies from drilling offshore. However, the oil companies abandoned the wells when they determined that the operations were not profitable given the price of oil at the time.

Oil company interest in offshore drilling has resurfaced in recent decades, especially in the late 1980s and again in 2008 as oil prices increased. In 1981 the federal government sold drilling leases to four companies: Mobil, Marathon, Chevron, and Conoco. In 1982 the Mineral Management Service (an agency with the Department of the Interior) approved a Chevron plan to explore Manteo block 510, an area northeast of Cape Hatteras. Chevron estimated that the Manteo Project site could produce as much as 1.5 billion barrels of oil or 5 trillion cubic feet of natural gas. If projections were correct, the site would have been one of the largest gas fields in the world. However, some estimated that the chance of a success-ful well was as low as 2 percent.[29]

Many Outer Banks residents worried that oil spills could cause signifi-cant environmental and economic damage. Even without drilling, unsightly oil wells off the coast, rampant industrial development, or increased tanker traffic could cause damage to the tourism industry. The proposed drilling site, known as "The Point," is the area where the warm Gulf Stream flowing from the south and the cold Labrador current flowing from the north collide. An oil spill in this popular recreational fishing area off Cape Hatteras would be very costly. In addition to lost revenues from fishery ground closings, commercial fisheries would suffer lost revenue owing to fewer fish and lower prices for their fish because of consumer concerns about contamination. For example, after an oil spill, Rhode Island spent hundreds of thousands of dollars in advertising to assure consumers that fish were safe to eat.

Although there has never been a major oil spill from drilling off the North Carolina coast, with the tourism industry such a large part of the local economy, the potential costs of an oil spill could be devastating.[30] There are two to three oil spills per year from the type of drilling that Chevron proposed, although most of the spills cause little harm.[31] However, an oil spill along the Outer Banks might not cause problems for tourism in the larger region because tourists may move to other coastal areas; for example, tourists may avoid the Outer Banks but may visit nearby Wrightsville Beach.

The timing of a spill could be a key determinant of how much effect an oil spill has on lost tourism revenues. If the spill occurs in the summer during the tourist season, for example, costs could be much higher than if the spill occurred in the winter. An oil spill in Rhode Island in January 1996—the slowest time of year for tourism—actually increased hotel and restaurant sales because workers arrived for the cleanup effort. However, a spill along the Texas coast in August 1979—during the busy tourist season—caused $3.1 to 3.8 million in lost revenues from tourists.[32]

A coalition of interests—members of which were opponents on other issues—fought the offshore drilling projects along the Outer Banks. Environmental organizations such as the Surfrider Foundation, commercial fishers, the tourism industry, and the state of North Carolina joined to oppose the drilling. In 1990, before any drilling could begin, Congress passed (and President George H. W. Bush signed) the Outer Banks Protection Act, which barred future oil exploration off the Outer Banks. Mobil and Marathon said that the law nullified their leases, and they sought compensation through a suit filed in Federal Claims Court in January 1995. In June 2000 the U.S. Supreme Court ruled 8–1 in favor of Mobil/Marathon that a "taking" had occurred and ordered the government to pay each company $78 million. Both companies agreed to give up their rights to drill. The twenty-year battle ended November 2000 when Conoco, the last oil company to retain drilling leases, relinquished the last eight leases that allowed offshore drilling.[33]

Public opinion was an important factor in Conoco's decision to halt offshore drilling. As a Conoco representative acknowledged, "All of the leases on the East Coast have been . . . very controversial. It was quite frankly not worth the effort."[34] Unfortunately public opinion can change. President William J. Clinton signed a temporary moratorium in June 1998 that withdrew all unleased areas in the Atlantic outer continental shelf from oil drilling through June 2012. However, on July 15, 2008, President George W. Bush, emboldened by the public outcry over four dollars a gallon for gasoline, lifted the moratorium. Although there is some public support for offshore drilling, there is some question as to whether it will occur. Indeed, because any oil produced would be only a small percentage of U.S. oil consumption and would not be available for five to ten years, offshore oil drilling would be a poor solution to current U.S. oil prices. However, when the price of a barrel of oil is in excess of one hundred dollars, offshore drilling would be profitable for oil companies.

Severe Weather

The United States might experience the greatest amount of extreme weather in the world. Three-fourths of the world's twisters, lightning strikes along the Rockies, blizzards, droughts, and floods all plague the country. David Laskin contends that geography, ocean currents, and global atmospheric circulation patterns make extreme weather the norm in the United States.[35] The Outer Banks gets some of the worst of it, especially when it comes in the form of hurricanes and northeasters. A favored location for hurricanes is Cape Hatteras, which juts out into the Atlantic. More hurricanes strike the Outer Banks than any other section of the U.S. coastline. Since 1585 at least 150 hurricanes have battered the Outer Banks; that is an average of 1 hurricane every 2.75 years.

Before the twentieth century, although many storms would have struck the Outer Banks, the reporting of storms was incomplete. Of the nineteenth-century storms, two of the most damaging may have been the 1842 and 1846 hurricanes; the latter changed the history of Portsmouth Island and will be discussed in a later chapter. Historically one of the strongest storms to strike the Outer Banks may have been the August 1899 hurricane, which at the time was the "worst one old folks could remember."[36] The storm was especially damaging on Shackleford Banks, where the overwash covered the entire island, killed most big trees, caused serious shore-line erosion, and washed many houses off their foundations. The whaling community of Diamond City, located on Shackleford Banks, was founded in 1885. Following the storm many of the five hundred residents tore their houses down board by board and moved to areas nearby, such as Harkers Island. By 1902 the entire population of Diamond City had packed up and moved, never to return.

The last major hurricane (that is, a Category 3, 4, or 5 on the Saffir-Simpson scale) to strike the Outer Banks was Emily, which was a Category 3 with winds of 115 mph. Emily, which luckily did not make landfall, gave the Outer Banks a glancing strike in 1993. The eye wall passed over Cape Hatteras before moving back to the east-northeast and out to sea. Blake and coauthors predict that a major hurricane will strike the Outer Banks on average every eleven years.[37] It would seem that a major hurricane is overdue, and the next one could make landfall, unlike Emily. If a Category 5 hurricane, with winds of 155 mph and a 15- to 18-foot storm surge, does

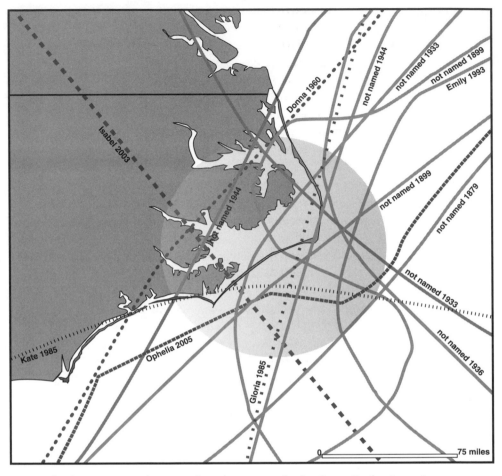

The fourteen most damaging hurricanes to strike the Outer Banks since 1879

strike the Outer Banks, a complete rebuilding of communities will be necessary.

One recent destructive storm, Hurricane Isabel, which came ashore on September 18, 2003, severely damaged the Outer Banks. Isabel cut a new 150-yard-wide inlet between Hatteras and Frisco, which was the first new inlet on the island since 1962. The U.S. Army Corps of Engineers and the North Carolina Department of Transportation filled the inlet with sand and rebuilt the damaged Highway 12. Isabel was able to stay at the highest level a hurricane can reach for more than thirty hours, which made it one of the longest lasting Category 5 storms on record. It eventually weakened to a Category 2 hurricane when it came ashore.

In the mid– to late twentieth century, hurricanes were in the headlines a lot. Hazel (1954), Hugo (1989), Andrew (1992), and Fran (1996) were the worst hurricanes ever to bedevil the eastern U.S. coast. Andrew and Hugo were the second and sixth most costly hurricanes of all time, although any one of the four could claim to be *the* storm of the twentieth century. We will not see another hurricane with one of these four names menacing a coastal community again because meteorologists retire the names of major hurricanes such as this costly group. However, the first decade of the twenty-first century has witnessed hurricanes that challenge this infamous quartet.

Perhaps the 2004 hurricane season with the costly Charley, Frances, Ivan, and Jeanne is a harbinger of upcoming years. The four hurricanes, which struck from the middle of August to the end of September, ravaged the state of Florida. In less than a month and a half Charley, Frances, and Jeanne traversed the Sunshine State battering interior and coastal areas. In some cases all three hurricanes hit the same communities. Of the four, Ivan was the strongest at Category 5, with the sixth lowest pressure ever recorded in the Atlantic at 910 millibars. Ivan would eventually weaken to a Category 3 prior to making landfall at Pensacola. In total the 2004 season offered fifteen named storms, nine hurricanes, and six major hurricanes, which caused more than $40 billion dollars in damage.

The following season was just as infamous and even more memorable. By the time the catastrophic 2005 season ended, a record twenty-seven named storms and fourteen hurricanes had formed, including Katrina, which may become the most memorable storm of the twenty-first century. On August 29, 2005, Katrina made landfall near Buras, Louisiana, and although only a Category 3 when the eye passed just east of New Orleans, it ranks as one of the costliest natural disasters in U.S. history.[38] The storm, which caused at least twelve hundred deaths, was especially damaging to New Orleans, where much of the city lies below sea level. Breaches in the flood-protection levees left 80 percent of New Orleans underwater, and perhaps three-quarters of all the houses in the city were destroyed or damaged. Following the hurricane governments' inept and sluggish responses—especially that of the Federal Emergency Management Agency—exacerbated the storm's impact.

After a period of infrequent hurricane activity between 1971 and 1994, the cycle of hurricane activity appears to have increased in the past decade. The five most intense consecutive storm seasons on record occurred between 1995 and 2000. An average of three storms per decade struck North Carolina from the 1950s through the 1970s. However, in the 1980s and 1990s six and seventeen storms, respectively, hit the state.[39] For the period from

2000 to 2004 an average of 4 per season struck the southeastern coast, compared to the average of 1.8 per year between 1970 and 1999. In addition hurricane forecasters at Colorado State University have predicted that this increased activity will continue for the next ten to forty years.[40] The researchers explain that simultaneous increases in North Atlantic sea-surface temperatures and decreases in vertical wind shear are causing the increased hurricane activity. However, there may be other reasons why we have been hearing so much about hurricanes recently.

Three factors may explain why many perceive that the risks from hurricanes are increasing. One possible explanation is that a rising sea level is increasing the risk of flooding in coastal areas. Sea level has been rising about a foot per century since the last ice age ended twenty thousand years ago. A second possible reason that might explain the perception of increasing risks from hurricanes is that the "CNN syndrome" artificially heightens hurricane visibility. With information-age technology we have a greater capability to report and document natural disasters such as hurricanes. News reporters scramble to capture the audience's attention with sensational headlines and stories. The Weather Channel, whose sole focus is the weather, provides in-depth coverage and analysis of every stage of a hurricane. Many of today's hurricanes may not be any more destructive than past ones, but we hear and see a lot more about each event.

A third factor that has created greater attention for hurricanes is that the damage costs from hurricanes are increasing. Hurricane Diane, which came ashore at Carolina Beach, North Carolina, in August 1955 and caused widespread flooding in the northeastern United States, was the first billion-dollar storm. The 2004 and 2005 hurricane seasons produced seven of the ten costliest insured losses to affect the United States, including those from Katrina, the most costly, which caused $45.3 billion in damages (see table 4.1). In total the seven hurricanes caused $79.3 billion in insured losses. In North Carolina seven of the ten costliest storms occurred in the 1990s; the ten costliest storms have all occurred since 1984. Floyd (in September 1999) and Fran (in September 1996), which caused $1.4 and $1.3 billion, respectively, are numbers one and two.

However, the increase in damage costs does not mean necessarily that storms have become more damaging in recent years. Pielke and his colleagues normalize previous storm damage by adjusting for inflation, wealth, housing, and population. Using this method the scientists estimate that a hurricane that struck Miami and did an *actual* $105 million damage in 1926 would have caused a *normalized* $150 billion in damages if it had struck in 2005; this made the 1926 storm more damaging than 2005's Katrina, which was number two on the list.[41] Indeed of the top ten most damaging storms

The ten costliest U.S. hurricanes

Rank	Date	Name	Cost in Millons of Dollars at Occurrence	Cost in Millions of 2008 Dollars*
1	August 25–29, 2005	Katrina	40,600	45,309
2	August 23–24, 25–26, 1992	Andrew	15,500	23,786
3	October 24, 2005	Wilma	10,300	11,355
4	September 12–14, 2008	Ike	11,700	11,700
5	August 13–15, 2004	Charley	7,475	8,520
6	September 16–21, 2004	Ivan	7,110	8,104
7	September 17–18, 21–22, 1989	Hugo	4,195	7,284
8	September 20–26, 2005	Rita	5,000	6,203
9	September 5, 2004	Frances	4,595	5,237
10	September 15–25, 2004	Jeanne	3,440	4,166

*Property coverage only
Source: Insurance Information Institute.

only two—Katrina and Andrew—occurred after 1969. Although we have no name for the 1926 storm that ravaged Miami (because prior to 1950 hurricanes were not given names), it remains a historical storm to remember.

Although storms may have been just as damaging in previous decades, the *actual* damage costs have increased. The principal causes of increased damage costs from hurricanes are more people building more expensive homes in hazard-prone areas. Insured property in hurricane-risk areas along the U.S. coast is valued at $2 trillion.[42] Each new major storm has the potential to become the most damaging storm ever because more homes that become increasingly expensive are built near the shore. The trend of increasing coastal development will continue to cause increasing costs from hurricanes—especially when calculated in dollars. Certainly the booming real-estate values on the Outer Banks in recent decades provide the potential dollars of damage from the next hurricane that makes landfall.

Whatever the causes of the increased storm damage costs in recent years, the increased payouts that insurance companies have experienced because of hurricane damage in the past two decades have led to dramatic changes in wind-insurance cost and availability. In Florida, for example, the average wind-insurance premium increased from $723 to $1,465 from 2002 to 2007, and in Florida's coastal areas premiums have tripled or even quadrupled.[43] Insurance rates in North Carolina's coastal areas increased by 90 percent from 2002 to 2008.[44] Flood-insurance premiums, which the NFIP establishes, have not changed as much as wind-insurance rates. The average flood-insurance premium for southeastern states in 2007 was $452, less than the national average of $510. In addition to increasing premiums, insurance companies have reduced their exposure in coastal areas. In Mississippi, State Farm, the largest insurer in the state, stopped selling new policies in February 2007. Some insurance companies have ceased including wind coverage in their standard policies for properties located in areas designated by the state as "wind pool areas."

States are becoming increasingly involved in providing wind insurance as insurance premiums have risen. All southeastern coastal states have set up state-run windstorm underwriters associations, referred to as "wind pools," which offer coverage from wind damage where private insurance is not available or is available only at very high rates. Some state legislatures are increasing government's role in coastal insurance markets, as in Florida's 2007 bill. Florida made a dramatic insurance policy change in 2007 with the Insurance Company Accountability and Regulatory Reform Act, which allows the state insurance company to compete directly with private insurers. The State's Citizens Property Insurance now accounts for more than one-third of all property insurance but a much higher percentage of high-risk coastal exposures.[45] At the federal level there continue to be calls for increased involvement in property insurance markets. In January 2007 the U.S. House of Representatives introduced the Homeowners' Insurance Protection Act, which would authorize the creation of an agency that would help finance residential losses that exceed the state fund capacity.

Hurricanes receive increased attention because of the combination of sea-level rise, increased coastal development, and media coverage. However, in years past hurricanes (except for Katrina) caused many more deaths than they do today. Historically storm surge, which is the wind-driven rise of the water, was responsible for most hurricane-related deaths. Storm surge, which can be twenty feet with a very strong hurricane, has accounted for 90 percent of the deaths from hurricanes—mostly through drowning. Storm surge killed most of the twelve thousand people who perished in the hurricane of 1900 that devastated Galveston, Texas.[46] Although hurricanes could cause severe damage inland, most deaths occur in coastal areas, which are most susceptible to storm surge.

With today's advanced warning of an approaching hurricane, residents who heed authorities are in little life-threatening danger. Now few lives are lost to storm surge. Over the past one hundred years, while the annual damages from hurricanes have increased from $210 million to more than $3 billion, the number of average annual deaths has dropped from more than one hundred to fewer than twenty.[47] The key to protecting human lives is to evacuate people before rising water makes it impossible to leave. This may be a challenge on the Outer Banks—especially if there are large numbers of tourists to move off the islands. Given the limited evacuation routes, the tendency for routes to be flooded before hurricane landfall, and the large number of tourists on the islands for much of the hurricane season, effective evacuation should be a priority concern for FEMA and other agencies.

Many of the new residents and visitors in coastal areas have experienced little of the destructive force of hurricanes. In recent decades during most of the period of rapid population growth in many coastal areas, fewer major hurricanes have affected coastal areas. Between 1966 and 1997, only five hurricanes struck the East Coast. By comparison, between 1940 and 1966, seventeen major hurricanes hit the East Coast. An apparent reversal in this trend is dispelling any false sense of security that some people may have, especially those who have lived on the Outer Banks for only a few years.

Hurricanes cost lives and money but also disrupt communities in other ways. Little public attention is directed toward coastal storm costs such as disruption of family life, stress resulting from loss of homes, health costs, and interruption to businesses. In addition hurricanes damage natural resources, eroding shorelines and destroying wildlife and wildlife habitats. For example, Hurricane Hugo destroyed 63 percent of the endangered red-cockaded woodpeckers in South Carolina's Francis Marion National Forest.

Although hurricanes capture more of the headlines, northeasters, which are more frequent, bigger, and last longer than hurricanes, can cause even greater damage to coastal property. Storm surge and waves, which can pound the shore for days, do most of the damage to shorelines. The 1962 Ash Wednesday storm, the most destructive northeaster of the twentieth century, destroyed or damaged hundreds of houses from north Florida to Massachusetts. The storm struck during extra-high tides, which brought storm waves much further onto the Outer Banks. The storm cut an inlet at Buxton, which required several attempts before engineers were able to close the inlet.

Erosion, Sea-Level Rise, and Climate Change

Shore-line erosion and sea-level rise create continuing concerns for many coastal communities. Shore-line erosion, which averages two to three feet per year along the Atlantic coast and six feet per year on the gulf coast, presents a persistent threat to coastal communities.[48] The average annual erosion rate on the Outer Banks, despite the Depression-era stabilization project, is approximately six feet, although between Avon and Buxton it is seventeen feet.[49] In addition sea level, which has changed frequently, is rising at about one foot per century. Both forces threaten the sustainability of many areas on the Outer Banks.

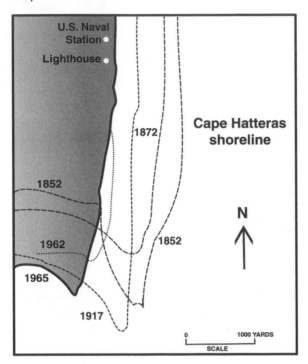

Shore-line recession along Cape Hatteras from 1852 to 1965. Created from historical maps and aerial photographs, this graphic illustrates the changeable nature of barrier islands. Courtesy of U.S. Army Corps of Engineers

Climate change will exacerbate the effects of both sea-level rise and erosion and provide special challenges for the Outer Banks and other coastal communities; many of the challenges will occur over the next fifty years. Although climate change occurs naturally, human activities have created conditions that cause more rapid changes. The burning of fossil fuels (the principal contributor to greenhouse gases) and the creation of other greenhouse gases (GHCs) create a greenhouse effect around the planet. The GHCs trap some of the infrared radiation, which would otherwise escape into space, in the troposphere (the lowest layer of the earth's atmosphere). Although some amount of the greenhouse effect is necessary for humans to survive, the current, rapid buildup of GHCs is causing world temperatures to increase to levels that will create severe problems for humankind.

A recent Intergovernmental Panel on Climate Change (IPCC) study projects that the increased level of GHCs will cause worldwide temperatures to increase by 1.1 to 6.4°C (2.0 to 11.5°F) by 2100. Curbing the actions that contribute to climate change will be doubly important for many coastal residents. The increase in temperatures from climate change will melt polar ice caps and cause a more rapid rise in sea level, which would flood some coastal areas and expose areas farther inland to wind and water damage. The IPCC assessment report projects that the sea level may increase by 1.5 to 2.6 feet above mean modern sea level by 2100.[50] Other recent reports suggest that the sea-level increase could be as much as 4.6 feet.[51] The concern is real enough that the National Association of Insurance Comissioners voted in March 2009 to require insurers to submit annual climate-risk reports that disclose the risks to insurers' portfolios from climate change.

Increasing sea-level rise creates numerous problems for coastal areas, such as more rapid erosion.[52] The sea-level increase will inundate many coastal areas, such as Miami Beach, New Orleans, and Hampton, Virginia.[53] The topography of the North Carolina coast, and in particular the Outer Banks, makes the area one of the most susceptible in the United States to climate change. Geologists have concluded that large portions of the Outer Banks could disappear within the next several decades if sea level continues to increase at the current level or if one or more major hurricanes directly hit the Outer Banks.[54]

As sea level rises and floods estuaries, which are important nurseries for fisheries, fish stocks will diminish. The U.S. commercial fishing industry, which contributed ($28 billion in 2001) to the Gross Domestic Product, is important to the U.S. economy. Sea-level rise will increase shore-line erosion, which will dampen tourism and recreational fishing, important elements of the Outer Banks economy. The National Marine Fisheries Service reports that North Carolina has 2.2 million recreational fishers, which is the second most saltwater anglers in the country. A recent study estimates that the loss to North Carolina's recreational fishing because of sea-level rise reducing beach width would be $1.26 billion over seventy-five years.[55] Sea-level rise will affect ground-water supplies and destroy coastal wetlands.

In addition expectations are that climate change will increase hurricane intensity, occurrence, and landfall frequency.[56] The theory explains that as the planet retains more heat, more air moves across the earth's surface providing higher wind speeds and more clashing warm and cold fronts, which are prime ingredients for hurricane activity. However, there is some debate on this issue. An alternative study theorizes that hurricane activity will decrease as temperatures warm.[57] The researchers argue that a difference in water temperatures between the tropical Atlantic and other basins, which have not warmed as quickly, has caused the increase in recent hurricane activity. The scientists predict that storm frequency may decline as the temperatures of the other basins catch up to the Atlantic, although the storms may produce more rain.

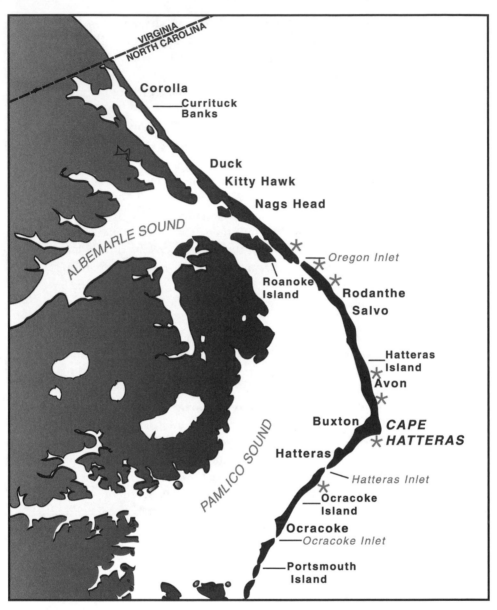

The seven asterisks on this map indicate Outer Banks locations that, based on geomorphology, have "very high" to "high" vulnerability to sea-level rise. From E. R. Thieler and E. S. Hammar-Klose, *National Assessment of Coastal Vulnerability to Future Sea-Level Rise* (1999)

A recent study examined some impacts that the increase in sea-level rise and hurricane activity caused by climate change would have on three segments of North Carolina's coastal economy—the real-estate market, recreation and tourism, and business activity.[58] The researchers estimate partial costs to the North Carolina coastal real-estate industry, tourism, and recreational fishing resulting from coastal erosion caused by sea-level rise. They predict that erosion will cause $3.2 and $3.7 billion of residential and non-residential losses, respectively, in the four counties of Bertie, New Hanover, Carteret, and Dare. With the loss of real estate, property taxes, which are an important source of revenue for the economy, would decrease. The cost to the southern North Carolina beaches' recreation and tourism industries from the shore-line erosion created by sea-level rise would be $3.9 billion.

In addition the researchers estimate the cost to some business activity—agriculture, forestry, and general "business interruption"—from increased storm severity. The increased cost to the North Carolina agriculture and forestry industries from a Category 2 hurricane or a Category 3 hurricane would be $1.5 billion. The cost on economic output owing to business interruption from 2030 to 2080 will vary, but the researchers estimate that cost would be $946 million for New Hanover County and a combined $496 million for Dare and Carteret counties.

Coastal areas can be precarious places to live. Hurricanes, northeasters, sea-level rise, and shore-line erosion can threaten and damage property. Climate change, which will cause an increase in sea-level rise and potentially more damaging hurricanes, will create even greater challenges for coastal communities. Despite the dangers, people are drawn to the shore, and in recent decades coastal populations have soared in many areas, including the Outer Banks. Population growth can exacerbate coastal problems, especially when the "tragedy of the commons" occurs. When access to a valuable resource is not limited and many wish to use the resource, the resource tends to be misused.

Growth will continue along the Outer Banks in coming decades regardless of the risks involved. That is good for many because the Outer Banks economy depends on the people who visit and move to the area. However, because the ecosystems along coastlines can be sensitive to developmental pressures, policy makers should implement programs that attempt to control the negative effects from development. Unfortunately policy makers subsidize some of the development that we wish to control. In a later chapter ways to live with the Outer Banks without destroying the beauty and uniqueness of the area are considered.

Five

Attempts at Controlling Change by Nature

The ravages committed by man subvert the relations and destroy the balance which nature had established between her organized and her inorganic creatures; and she avenges herself on the intruder, by letting loose on her defaced provinces destructive energies hitherto kept in check by organic forces destined to be his best auxiliaries, but which he has unwisely dispersed and driven from the field of action.

George Perkins Marsh

The forces of nature are similar in some ways to forces that operate in the market economy. The market system does a great balancing act of allocating scarce resources to the uses that society values most highly. In the marketplace consumers and producers act independently to determine the market equilibrium price. Consumers, who decide how much they are willing to pay, and producers, who decide how much they are willing to accept, set the market price for a product. If consumers wish to buy more than firms are producing currently, then prices rise in order to bring more supply into the market. If prices are higher than consumers are willing to pay, a product will be left on the shelf until prices fall, which will encourage more consumers to buy the product. Equilibrium occurs between producers and consumers when no participant has any reason to alter his or her behavior. Supply equals demand, and the market remains in equilibrium until some event causes market participants to alter their decisions.

Governments sometimes attempt to manipulate equilibrium prices for a variety of reasons. When a 1954 Supreme Court decision forced the federal government to limit how high natural-gas prices could rise, producers could not afford to supply as much gas as consumers desired at the restricted prices. Although consumers who could get the inexpensive gas were pleased, by the winter of 1974–75 some parts of the country were unable to get natural gas *at any price.* In the northeastern United States, for example, the shortage forced businesses and schools to close when they were unable to get natural gas. The price controls had created an inefficient and unfair situation. The government began phasing out price controls in 1978, and although prices rose initially, the shortage was eliminated.

Although rulers and governments have tried to subvert the laws of supply and demand throughout history, inevitably they have failed. They have learned that trying to control the market's powerful forces is futile and costly. Government has tried to control nature's forces, especially in coastal areas where wind and wave create outcomes that dissatisfy humans. The attempts to control nature, however, often create consequences that are at least as undesirable as the original problem.

Changing Inlets

Inlets seek equilibrium and adjust for changing conditions, just as markets do. Rising tides transport water through the inlets into the sounds, and falling tides transport the water back through. Inlets move sand from the front of the beach to the sound side, which helps with the process of island transgression. In addition, inlets can minimize the damage from storms by providing valuable release points for water. When hurricane-created storm surge rushes back to the sea, inlets provide the path of least resistance. Although inlets are part of nature's balancing act, the changing patterns of inlets can frustrate boaters, who find it difficult to navigate inlets that shift and shoal. In addition, inlets, which tend to move laterally, can erode shorelines and destroy property. For these reasons humankind attempts to dredge and stabilize inlets.

The first attempt at shore-line engineering along the Outer Banks was in 1830, when the Army Corps of Engineers began dredging Ocracoke Inlet, which was an important passageway for the lightering industry.[1] Concerned that Ocracoke Inlet could fill completely, the ACE used a steam-driven dredging machine to deepen and widen the inlet. After seven years of dredging failed to produce any success, because the inlet filled in as fast as it was dredged, engineers began constructing a jetty. In 1837, when a storm destroyed the uncompleted jetty, the ACE abandoned the project.

Failure at the first shore-line engineering attempt did not discourage humans from undertaking other projects that tried to bend nature to the wishes of humankind. With improved technology the efforts have become more powerful but no more successful. In 1971 the ACE used dynamite to blast New Drum Inlet through the Core Banks in order to provide a faster route for boats from the sound to the ocean. However, the dynamite caused the inlet to widen and shoal, which made it useless for boat traffic. Although the ACE dredged the new inlet, it was not able to keep the passageway from shoaling and abandoned this project as well.[2]

The most controversial inlet project on the Outer Banks has been the plan to stabilize Oregon Inlet. Oregon Inlet separates Bodie and Hatteras islands and is the only barrier-island break in the northern part of the Outer Banks. The inlet, which was created by the 1846 hurricane, is less stable than the other two inlets (Hatteras and Ocracoke) that provide access to Pamlico Sound. Longshore currents cause the inlet to migrate in a southerly direction (which is the normal pattern for Outer Banks inlets) by about one hundred feet a year.[3] In addition the combination of currents and wave action causes sand to settle in the inlet. When the state constructed the Herbert C. Bonner Bridge across the inlet in 1963, the natural movement of the inlet stopped, and the situation worsened. As the inlet began to clog with sand, the Army Corps of Engineers began annual dredgings of the inlet in order to allow navigation of the channel. However, ACE engineers envisioned a more ambitious project that they claimed would be a permanent solution—twin mile-long jetties that would be 200 feet wide at the underwater base and rise 10 feet above the waves. Engineers believed that the jetties, construction of which was estimated to cost between $80 million and $120 million, would stop sand from flowing into and clogging the inlet.[4] In December 1970 Congress authorized the jetties' construction. As part of the project the North Carolina Department of Transportation built a controversial 3,150-foot "terminal groin" in 1989 at a cost of $16 million.[5]

Commercial fishers and charter boat operators were the primary advocates of the stabilization project (in addition to the Army Corps of Engineers) because the inlet's shifting shoals made passage for boats treacherous. Supporters of the project maintained that the jetties would be a boon to the local economy (especially to fishers based in the Wanchese community on Roanoke Island) because fishers would be able to traverse the inlet more easily and therefore increase catches. The state of North Carolina, which completed construction of the Seafood Industrial Park at Wanchese in May 1981 in order to attract seafood-processing firms and create jobs and income, was looking forward to increased landings as well. In addition supporters contended that the jetties would decrease the erosion on Pea Island because sand that would otherwise be trapped in the inlet would flow to the island instead.[6] Economic impact studies by the ACE showed that the benefits would exceed the costs of the project.

Some, however, voiced concerns about the project. A group of coastal scientists, environmentalists, and National Park Service officials questioned whether the ACE had considered the potentially damaging environmental consequences of the jetties on the Cape Hatteras National Seashore and the Pea Island National Wildlife Preserve. In 1979 the Department of

Interior created a panel of several coastal scientists and engineers (the Inman Panel, as it became known) to review the ACE's plans and to determine whether the concerns were legitimate. The panel's four reports (completed in 1979, 1980, 1987, and 1991) questioned the basic concepts behind the ACE's plans. One conclusion of the panel was that the jetties would increase, not decrease, erosion by blocking sand that would normally nourish beaches on Pea and Hatteras islands. In addition the panel found that the ACE minimized the effect that sea-level rise might have on the project and dismissed the dredging-only alternative without sufficient consideration.[7]

The National Marine Fisheries Service (NMFS), another federal agency, raised an additional concern about the jetties' impacts. The agency worried that the jetties would block the fish, shrimp, and crab larvae that hatch at sea and are swept through the inlet into the sound. The result would be reduced fish populations, creating additional problems for a resource that had been overfished already. In addition, because ocean fisheries had been depleted already, the NMFS noted that increased fish landings for the Wanchese community were unlikely. Thus a principal reason for the project and a major contributor to the economic benefits estimation appeared to be invalid.

Ken Hunter, a private consultant, raised another objection to the project. Hunter discovered that the ACE had greatly inflated the economic benefits of the increased nontraditional fish (such as squid, mackerel, and sea herring) that would be caught. When Hunter adjusted the ACE's benefit-cost ratio, he estimated that the project costs were three times greater than the benefits.[8] The ACE adjusted the benefit-cost ratio to account for the error but maintained that the jetties were cost-efficient and environmentally sound. Despite the many concerns, the continued backing of Senator Jesse Helms made the jetty construction likely. In June 2000 Helms maneuvered to transfer land that was needed for the jetty construction to the Army Corps of Engineers.[9]

More than three decades after the birth of the plan, an administration concerned with cost cutting deep-sixed the Oregon Inlet jetties. In May 2003 the Bush administration cut the ACE budget and froze new construction, effectively halting the controversial project.[10] The White House Council on Environmental Quality mediated the dispute between two federal agencies, the Army Corps of Engineers and the National Marine Fisheries Service. As White House Council on Environmental Quality chairman James Connaughton explained, "Working with the Army and the other agencies, we looked closely at the economic and environmental data and jointly determined that the uncertainties in projecting both the estimated

Bonner Bridge spanning Oregon Inlet, which was opened by a hurricane in 1846.
The plan to stabilize the inlet was a contentious issue for many years.

economic and environmental effect, and the risk to important resources,
weigh against proceeding with the project."[11] The agencies concluded that
it was questionable whether the project would generate even moderate net
benefits. In addition the agencies agreed that because of the decline in fish
stocks, it was unlikely that the jetties would lead to increased fish landings.
The new policy directed the ACE to improve the navigation channel (by
dredging) and provide up-to-date navigational data on the channel conditions.

The bridge over Oregon Inlet continues to be a contentious issue. The
Bonner Bridge, which was built in 1963, had a life expectancy of thirty years
and must be replaced. Two plans, both of which are costly (perhaps one
billion dollars or more) and subject to complications, have been considered.[12] One option is to build a bridge that would parallel the old 2.5-mile
bridge and maintain the Pea Island road on its present right of way. However, the Pea Island road is expected to require either elevation or reloca-
tion within the lifetime of the new bridge. The second option is a longer
bridge, about 17 miles southward through shallow Pamlico Sound and ending at Rodanthe on Hatteras Island. Depending on which plan officials
approve, negative impacts to nearby ecosystems may need to be considered.
The recent discovery of a deed that would allow the U.S. Department of
Transportation to relocate the existing roadway south of the inlet makes
the shorter bridge more likely.[13]

A photograph taken from the top of the Cape Hatteras Lighthouse (silhouetted on the shore) shows the zigzag line of slatted fencing erected by CCC and WPA workers to build sand dunes. Courtesy of the National Park Service, Cape Hatteras National Seashore

Erosion and Dune Stabilization Revisited

Shore-line erosion is a gradual but persistent event generally. Wind and wave action, barrier-island transgression, and human activity all contribute to shore-line erosion, which is always present on the Outer Banks. In 1986 the North Carolina Division of Coastal Management determined that 73 percent of the 237 miles of North Carolina oceanfront was eroding. The problem of shore-line erosion compelled planners to undertake the 1930s dune-stabilization project, which in turn spurred Outer Banks development. Initially the dune-stabilization project that created a wall of vegetated dunes paralleling the ocean from south of Nags Head to the southern end of Ocracoke was considered a success. In a 1940 report Stratton and Hollowell, the project's engineers, expressed a sense of vindication: "Many thought the idea of controlling the fast eroding shoreline by the use of flimsy brush fences and grass planting was preposterous. Now that the job is nearly completed there are practically no skeptics. The work has been more successful than had been hoped for. It is true that a large sum of money and man-hours and materials have been expended but the results more than justify all that has been spent."[14]

As expected, the artificial dunes prevented lowland flooding during major storms, and the vegetation reduced wind erosion. Stratton believed that the benefits from the artificial dunes would be substantial for Bankers:

> Much of the danger to their lives and property has been eliminated and security restored. . . . The danger of the highway being torn up by storms has been almost entirely eliminated. . . . the fresh water fishing industry has been restored . . . [because] the waters of the sound are again fresh. . . . The water fowl of this area, known the world over have greatly increased on account of the reclamation of fresh water areas and the resulting increase in feeding grounds. . . . Thousands of acres of timber and wooded lands have been saved from over-riding dunes. . . . Both Government and private property as well have been greatly increased in value as a result of this project. . . . In some instances abandoned Government property and buildings have been save [sic]. Among these are the Cape Hatteras Lighthouse. . . . There are many more benefits which have resulted from this work that are too numerous to mention.[15]

With such euphoric (although mistaken) reports, it was not surprising that the government continued the dune-protection program. In 1952 Park Service director Conrad L. Wirth promised in an open letter to the people of the Outer Banks that the Park Service would continue to "protect and control the sand dunes, to reestablish them when necessary, and hold them to protect the communities from the intrusion of the ocean."[16] In 1953 the dunes system was rebuilt and the dunes were extended to the park's southern boundary on Ocracoke Island.[17] However, only two decades later serious questions were raised about the erosion-control program.

In the early 1970s two researchers—Robert Dolan, a coastal geologist at the University of Virginia, and Paul Godfrey, a botanist from the University of Massachusetts—found evidence that rather than saving the islands, the 1930s-built dunes were adversely affecting the islands.[18] The researchers found that the artificial dune system was functioning differently from the precolonial dune system. Prior to the dune construction, wind and overwash carried sand to the sound side. The artificial dunes, which were higher than the precolonial dunes, prevented the natural process of overwash, sand movement, and plant succession. New salt marsh could not form on the sound side without the sand deposited by overwash, which allowed marsh grasses to grow. Without marsh grasses to buffer sound-side wave action, more erosion occurred on the sound side.

In addition the artificial dunes act much like a seawall that concentrates waves on the beach and creates a narrower beach. The artificial dunes caused the waves to bite into the beach so that sand that overwash normally carried to the sound-side beach remained on the ocean-front beach or was carried out to sea. The precolonial dunes allowed wave overwash, which allowed waves to dissipate their force over a larger area.[19] When Dolan and Godfrey compared the width of the natural beach against that of the altered beach, the harmful results of the dune stabilization were evident. On Core Banks, which was not altered, beaches were 400 to 650 feet wide, while on Hatteras Island, which was part of the stabilization project, beaches were only 100 feet wide and in some places almost completely eroded.[20] Thus, although the planners of the stabilization process successfully stopped the overwash, the project was a failure because the importance of island migration was not appreciated in the 1930s. As Dolan and coauthors explained, "natural disruptive change is often essential to the maintenance of ecosystem structure and function."[21]

Dolan and Godfrey's research removed an additional justification for dune stabilization. When the 1930s project was first proposed, many believed that humankind's activities, such as cutting trees and allowing livestock to roam freely, caused island deforestation and erosion. In an influential series of articles Frank Stick blamed humankind for deforesting the Outer Banks, which he claimed had been almost completely forested at one time.[22] Others before Stick, such as John Spears, provided accounts suggesting that the Outer Banks was once heavily forested, although the evidence for such assertions was unclear.[23] If the deforestation increased shore-line erosion, then it seemed appropriate to enact erosion-control measures that would restore the wooded landscape, protect the shoreline, and help resurrect the faltering Outer Banks economy. Indeed upon completion of the dune stabilization Stratton and Hollowell proudly proclaimed, "Instead of a barren sand swept stretch of beach it has been transformed to an area not unlike its original condition."[24]

However, Dolan and colleagues explain that the Outer Banks was never thickly forested but rather was covered with low-lying plants that could survive overwash and occasional flood tides from Pamlico Sound. Such vegetation survives as part of the process of island migration, which moves the island toward the mainland. The few permanent forests on the Outer Banks, such as the one at Buxton, developed only where relatively high back dunes formed near the sound. Dolan and colleagues note that earlier

researchers—some well before the dune-stabilization project was suggested—reached similar conclusions.[25]

Because of Dolan and Godfrey's research the National Park Service
(NPS) adopted a new policy of letting nature take its own course. In 1973
the NPS canceled a $4.5 million planned beach-nourishment project at
Buxton and began following a policy of allowing natural erosion. Orrin
Pilkey spurred national interest in the issue when he announced to a group
of journalists that the federal government had decided to let Buxton fall
into the sea.[26] Officials, in less dramatic fashion, described the new policy
in a 1974 document: "Following damaging storms, the dunes would not be
artificially rebuilt, but in extensive barren areas a revegetation program
would be initiated. . . . Inlets which opened during storms would be permitted to migrate and close naturally. . . . This alternative envisions that at
some time in the future it may be impractical to maintain a continuous
road throughout the seashore."[27]

The only exceptions to the hands-off policy were the protection of important historical landmarks (such as the Hatteras Lighthouse) and necessary infrastructure (such as state roads). Not everyone was happy with
the policy change. Many longtime residents felt betrayed by the National
Park Service, which had promised two decades before to "protect and control the sand dunes."

Dolan and Godfrey's research was instrumental in changing National
Park Service policy, but other factors contributed. The expense of continuing the erosion-control program was a problem for the NPS. When the
organization resumed dune construction in the late 1950s, control costs
increased beyond original expectations. By 1971 the NPS was spending
$500,000 a year to replenish sand. By 1973 the NPS had spent $20 million
on erosion control, and expectations were that costs would continue to
increase. In addition, when the NPS announced the policy change (which
became a national story in part because of Pilkey's dramatic statement),
media opinion agreed that it was time to stop protecting the beach from
natural forces. The increased environmental consciousness of the 1970s
may partially explain why newspaper editorials around the country were
supportive of the National Park Service (except for those close to the North
Carolina coast).[28]

In recent decades scientists have improved their understanding of
coastal dynamics and erosion. The combination of natural forces such as
sea-level rise, storm frequency, and overwash as well as human actions
make the erosion equation difficult to simplify. What is clear is that the
dune-stabilization project successfully lessened the effects of ocean overwash that the planners of the project mistakenly believed caused "a one

time haven of rest and beauty [to be] changed to a barren beach subject to the ravages of sand, water, and wind."[29]

However, Robert Burns's caution that even the best-laid plans often go astray applies to the stabilization project, which has created a dilemma for policy makers. The project did not solve erosion problems but created a false sense of security; the belief that the artificial dunes would protect infrastructure such as highways encouraged economic growth and rapid development. Indeed the project has exacerbated the problems of living on the Outer Banks because the construction project has increased erosion rates, creating increased threats to the expanding, densely developed communities. The constructed dunes, which prevent most overwash and less sediment to the barrier island's sound side, create increased rates of sound-side shore-line erosion just as hardened structures would. In addition the constructed dunes encourage a steeper ocean beach profile that increases the rate of shore-line recession.[30]

As the twenty-first century began, portions of the stabilized dunes were disappearing, and Kitty Hawk, Kill Devil Hills, Nags Head, Rodanthe, and other coastal towns have been facing severe beach-erosion problems. Although the present erosion rate along the Outer Banks of one meter per year is insignificant from a geological perspective, sand loss seriously threatens many ocean-front properties. Conditions along Kitty Hawk beaches illustrate the erosion problem. Although dunes constructed by the 1930s CCC project provided some property protection for a time, over the past two decades storm waves have repeatedly flooded property and washed out portions of roads.[31] The problem is most pressing for a section of Kitty Hawk where the dunes cannot be rebuilt because the sea has eroded the beach beyond the point where the dunes used to be. As some ocean-front homes begin to fall into the sea, Bankers may find that the promise of dune stabilization was but a short-lived vanity.

Moving the Cape Hatteras Lighthouse

As Dolan and Godfrey have shown, engineering solutions, such as the dune-stabilization project, that try to stop the powerful forces of wind and water are only temporary fixes at best, and at worst they create serious problems. The saga of the Cape Hatteras Lighthouse, which is a valued Cape Hatteras National Seashore attraction, illustrates the difficulty of using engineering techniques to battle natural forces. The Hatteras Lighthouse, which is painted with distinctive black and white spirals, is perhaps the most famous landmark on the North Carolina coast. Although the light no longer serves a maritime purpose, it is an important historic monument and a tourist favorite.

The Hatteras Lighthouse, which is 208 feet in height, is the tallest brick lighthouse in the United States. When it was built in 1870 to warn ships that they were approaching the shoals of the Graveyard of the Atlantic, the lighthouse stood 1,500 feet inland from the ocean waves. However, erosion gradually brought the waves closer and threatened the light. Resting on yellow pine timbers and a 3-foot base of granite rubble and masonry, the lighthouse could be undercut by storm waves. Officials tried two accepted engineering solutions to try slowing shore-line erosion—armoring and renourishing the beach. Armoring builds hard devices such as seawalls, and renourishment adds sand to the shore. Eventually a third approach emerged—retreat.

The government first attempted to protect the light in 1935 when the ocean was within 100 feet of the lighthouse; engineers constructed sheet-steel piling in front of the light. A short time later planners of the 1930s project completed the artificial dunes that they believed would provide additional protection for the lighthouse. However, by World War II ocean waves had nearly reached the light and threatened to topple it into the sea. In the 1960s and 1970s three groins were built and nylon sand-filled bags were stacked in front of the lighthouse. In 1966, using a "softer" approach, a government-funded beach-nourishment project pumped 312,000 cubic yards of sand on the shoreline. Other unsuccessful attempts by the government included slabs of asphalt, sand fences, and even artificial seaweed. Between 1935 and 1981 the National Park Service spent $15 million on the temporary solutions.[32] Eventually nature had its way.

In 1982, after a large winter storm almost knocked the lighthouse over, interested parties began serious debate over how best to save the structure. The possible options included allowing the lighthouse to succumb to the ocean, replenishing the sand, building a seawall, or moving the lighthouse. A panel of scientists from the National Academy of Engineering and the National Academy of Sciences concluded that moving the light was the best alternative. The Army Corps of Engineers, on the other hand, believed that building a seawall around the light and allowing it to become an island as the shoreline eroded around it would be the best choice.[33]

By the 1980s the National Park Service, after extended debates about how best to preserve the lighthouse, began making plans to relocate it. Many were not happy with the move. Some believed that the lighthouse would fall apart during the move, as expressed in a lawsuit by Dare County that referred to the proposal as a "disastrous American boondoggle." Others believed that even if successful, relocating the lighthouse away from the shoreline diminished its appeal. When Congress appropriated $9.8

Cape Hatteras Lighthouse before it was relocated. The National Park Service tried several engineering approaches, including sandbags and a groin, to protect the historic lighthouse from erosion.

The lighthouse in its new location. The National Park Service successfully moved the historic lighthouse sixteen hundred feet from the sea.

million for the move in 1998, park officials began planning the lighthouse's trip of more than a half mile.

The National Park Service began moving the light twenty-nine hundred feet to its new location on June 17, 1999. Engineers constructed a sophisticated system of steel beams and hydraulic ramps to relocate the structure. One hundred heavy-duty steel rollers, each capable of withstanding seventy-five tons of weight, were matched with hydraulic jacks. The rollers moved along seven travel beams, which leapfrogged ahead of the rolling platform. Seven hydraulic rams nudged the lighthouse along in five-foot strokes. At the speed of a garden slug, about 1½ inches per minute, engineers inched the light along a sandy track over a period of three weeks. Any potential problems would have been relayed by a series of sensors that continuously measured stresses and alignments and fed data to a computer. Successfully moving the forty-eight-hundred-ton beacon, which could have cracked or even fallen apart during the process, was an engineering marvel.[34]

The current location is sixteen hundred feet from the sea, about the same distance from ocean waves that the original light stood when it was built in 1870. Even this site is not permanent; in one hundred years, as the beach erodes, the sea will once again reach the light. For now, though, visitors can climb the 257 steps to the top of the lighthouse and appreciate the historical monument. By moving the lighthouse, the NPS solved the problem for a century and avoided the recurring costs of shore-line protection.

The Cape Hatteras Lighthouse is a metaphor for the human struggle to stop the forces of nature along shorelines. Although none of the numerous hurricanes that have hit the North Carolina coast has damaged the lighthouse's sturdy masonry walls, the persistent shore-line erosion eventually forced its retreat. The story of the Cape Hatteras Lighthouse illustrates that in some cases organized retreat from the shore may be the only solution to threats from the natural forces that affect shorelines.

A comparison of John White's 1585 map to a current map of the Outer Banks shows that the Outer Banks has migrated toward the mainland by thousands of feet in the past four hundred years. Policy makers from the 1930s misinterpreted the natural process of island translocation as human-caused erosion. An additional misconception that justified the dune-stabilization project was the notion that the Outer Banks had once been heavily forested. Although humankind has been responsible for some deforestation on the Outer Banks, it is now understood that natural "destructive" change (which is essential for an ecosystem to function) was the principal cause of the limited amount of vegetation there.

The engineers of the dune-stabilization project proved partially pro-phetic in this hopeful statement: "We who are familiar with the work have belief in its lasting benefits, although *time alone will be the judge* [italics added]."[35] Unfortunately it is the second half of the statement that has proved accurate.

Natural forces have confounded the best engineering efforts to stabilize inlets and shorelines. Human use of technology to control natural processes, such as shore-line erosion and inlet migration, that threaten property and profit can be costly and futile despite the varied technology that engineers have employed. Ironically sometimes the change creates more of a prob-lem, as was the case with the dune-stabilization project, which has in-creased erosion. It is clear that the belief that the stabilization process halted erosion encouraged the economic growth and rapid development of the Outer Banks in recent years. Today erosion is a more serious problem because of this development. In hindsight most would agree that a more controlled development would have been advisable.

Both the dune-stabilization and the Oregon Inlet projects were major government plans that were halted. Stopping such well-established pro-grams is difficult and not usually possible. Although both projects have been eliminated, the belief that nature can and should be controlled has not. The next project with better political support or a better benefit-cost ratio may be approved even when the outcome is questionable. The Hat-teras Lighthouse reminds us that although the current shoreline will retreat eventually, a beach will remain. The lesson might be that in order to coex-ist with the shore-line ecosystem, humankind may need to let nature take its course and do less engineering.

Six

Living with Change in
Coastal Communities

A thing is right when it tends to preserve the integrity, stability, and beauty of the biotic community. It is wrong when it tends otherwise.

Aldo Leopold

Physical processes such as storms, waves, and wind make coastlines some of the most changeable places on the earth's surface. The change caused by a particular force, such as the 1846 hurricane that struck Portsmouth Island, can be both immediate and deferred. Human activities can alter barrier islands as well. However, many of humankind's alterations are more predictable and the causes better understood than nature's forces. Therefore it is useful to search for policies that best minimize damage to coastal areas.

The rapid population increase in recent decades is responsible for many of the problems facing coastal communities. It is no surprise that people want to be near the natural beauty of land and sea to escape the congestion and hectic lifestyles of cities and suburbs. Unfortunately, as the mobile American population rushes to the shore, the intensive use of fragile coastal resources creates substantial damage. No one ever purposely sets out to pollute waters, destroy wildlife habitat, or create congested communities. We inadvertently damage the environment as we make choices about what to produce and where and how to live. For example, as developers build new communities, they alter and destroy some of the natural environment. Similarly in the production process, industry often uses the air, water, and land to dispose of waste.

Although it is not possible to have zero impact on the environment, we can collectively choose to minimize environmental pollution and harmful alterations. Humankind's actions can be difficult to control, but policymakers may be able to direct human activity to minimize the damage inflicted on coastal areas. The key is to alter incentive structures.

Controlling Coastal Development

Many coastal areas have become overdeveloped because so many people want to be at the beach. Unfortunately we have a limited amount of coastline. In areas adjacent to the U.S. coast, the population density is more than 230 persons per square mile—three times that of the nation as a whole.[1] Although the new residents and tourists may be good for the economy, larger populations can damage the environment and the quality of community life. This is not a new problem. So many Romans were crowding their shore in the sixth century that Emperor Justinian passed an ordinance prohibiting construction within one hundred feet of the shore to protect sea views. Fifteen centuries later we are still struggling to control coastal development, and we continue to use government regulation to rein in the problems created by having too many people at the beach.

Some Outer Banks communities have implemented policies to limit the negative impacts of growth. Nags Head, for example, has channeled growth to areas best suited for development in order to protect the aquifer that provides the island's water supply. Town planners discourage development in aquifer-recharge zones, wetlands, and areas most susceptible to natural disasters. Shore-line setbacks are farther from the beachfront than required by federal and state law. In addition planners limit the number of ocean-front condominiums and hotels by restricting building size. In the summer of 2003 local government planners set limits on house size and created guidelines for design in Nags Head, Southern Shores, Kill Devil Hills, Duck, and Kitty Hawk.[2]

Buxton Woods provides an example of how citizen activists can work with local government to preserve unique areas. In 1986 developers planned to build a new golf course and housing development in Buxton Woods, a unique maritime forest. Buxton Woods, which protects Hatteras Island's water supply, is the only heavily wooded area on the island. The development would have destroyed much of the forest, and the golf course would have required a large amount of the limited water supply on the island. Following months of negotiations the county commissioners adopted the island's first zoning code, and the state eventually purchased 450 acres of Buxton Woods in order to preserve the area. The towns of Kill Devil Hills and Pine Knoll Shores have followed the Buxton Woods example to protect valuable resources.[3]

In 1991 residents of Ocracoke instituted several policies to control development that would have changed the character of the community. The citizens barred new marinas and limited the development of coastal wetlands. In addition Ocracokers prohibited construction of a sewage-treatment plant because residents felt that the plant would spur undesirable economic development. Similarly the people of Manteo preserved the quality of their community by directing development to highlight the town's history and waterfront. Communities have tried a variety of other tools such

This row of ocean-front homes in Rodanthe illustrates
the danger of building in high-hazard areas.

as impact fees, transferable development rights, and conservation easements to minimize the costs of growth.

State governments, spurred on by the federal government, have implemented programs that regulate coastal area activities. The goals of the North
Carolina Coastal Area Management Act (CAMA) of 1974 are to reduce
storm and erosion damage and to protect coastal-area amenities.[4] CAMA
provides a plan to guide development in the twenty county coastal areas,
identifies areas of environmental concern (AEC), and institutes a permit

system to manage development in coastal areas. A fifteen-member Coastal Resources Commission, which formulates and oversees coastal policy, designates four types of AECs: 1) estuaries; 2) ocean hazard areas; 3) public water supplies; and 4) natural and cultural resource areas.

CAMA authorized the Division of Coastal Management to determine the distance that new development must be set back from the oceanfront. The agency creates set-back lines that locate structures at minimum distances from eroding shorelines in order to protect life, property, and public access. Single-family homes of 5,000 square feet or less must be thirty times the historical long-term erosion rate from the line of stable natural vegetation nearest the sea. Buildings that are greater than 5,000 square feet must be sixty times the long-term erosion rate (for example, 2 feet per year) or thirty times the long-term erosion rate plus 105 feet behind the line; the location that is closer to the ocean is chosen.

The North Carolina General Assembly has amended CAMA regularly. Although various groups have challenged CAMA in court, "the overall record of judicial review is one of solid support for CAMA and the agencies that administer it."[5] A 1992 study recognized CAMA as one of the nation's best coastal management programs.[6] However, special interest groups, such as the real-estate industry, may be able to manipulate policy and achieve outcomes that subvert coastal protection goals. Numerous examples illustrate that policies such as set-back requirements can be overturned in favor of more development and larger houses.[7] In a study of local planning in coastal North Carolina, Richard Norton found that although all twenty coastal counties were preparing plans consistent with state guidelines, the plans were weak and provided limited guidance for growth management, especially with regard to coastal-resource protection.[8]

The federal government regulates coastal activities as well. Three major pieces of legislation are the principal policies that have affected coastal development, although not always for the better. The 1968 National Flood Insurance Program, although meant to protect coastal areas, encourages more development by providing subsidized flood insurance. The goal of the Coastal Zone Management Act (CZMA) of 1973 is "to preserve, protect, develop, and where possible, to restore or enhance the resources of the nation's coastal zone." CZMA required states to prepare and implement coastal management programs, such as North Carolina's CAMA. The Coastal Barrier Resource Act (CBRA) of 1982, the third piece of legislation, withdrew federal assistance to 186 undeveloped coastal barrier islands along the Atlantic and Gulf coasts. CBRA prohibits federal funding for any construction of structures or infrastructure, stabilization projects, and federally subsidized flood insurance within these areas. Although not prohibiting construction, CBRA places the costs and risks of development on the private sector and those enjoying the benefits of coastal areas.

Government planning is no panacea, however. Growth controls often are ineffective because some groups desire more development. Groups that benefit from growth can influence policy makers and often limit the effectiveness of growth controls. Even when growth controls are effective, they may be only temporary. When economic growth slows, there are often calls for government to encourage economic development. A new set of government guidelines can offset a previous set of growth controls. Platt and his coauthors found widespread compliance with vertical regulations but uneven application of minimum setbacks. In addition they report that oceanfront structures are better built to resist wind and wave forces but that ongoing erosion continues to threaten development. They conclude that political pressures have often overwhelmed coastal regulation, especially CBRA.[9]

Events on Topsail Beach, just off the coast of Wilmington, North Carolina, illustrate this concern. Topsail's low elevation, narrowness, and limited offshore sand supply make it especially prone to storm damage. In 1954, for example, Hurricane Hazel covered the island with nine feet of water and destroyed or damaged all 210 structures there. Legislation has not limited development in high-hazard areas on the island. Although CBRA covers much of North Topsail, the state has built roads and bridges and issued permits for sewer plants and other infrastructure. In addition developers have constructed many new houses, some in high-hazard areas. In 1996 Hurricane Fran destroyed 320 buildings, roads, and bridges in addition to cutting new inlets across the island. In spite of the island's previous devastations, the state rebuilt the roads and bridges and filled in the new inlets.[10]

Government regulation may run into legal challenges, especially when that regulation reduces private property values and owners are not compensated, as was the case in the landmark challenge by David Lucas.[11] In 1988 the South Carolina legislature passed the Beachfront Management Act, which implemented set-back lines to limit construction too close to the shore. David Lucas, a land developer, challenged the state when the new law would not allow him to build houses on two Isle of Palms oceanfront lots he had bought in 1986. Lucas felt that the state had unfairly taken away the value of his property without compensating him. The state, because it did not take the Lucas property and was acting in the public interest, felt that compensation was not justified. Four years and several legal decisions later, the U.S. Supreme Court ordered South Carolina to compensate Lucas for the value of the property unless the state could prove that building the two houses would harm the public. South Carolina paid Lucas when the state supreme court ruled that the state failed to make a case that significant public harm would result.[12]

Often the conflict between the rights of property owners and providing for the public welfare is not easily settled. However, government agencies can avoid legal challenges from property owners by purchasing land as North Carolina did in the Buxton Woods case. In recent years many communities have voted to increase taxes in order to purchase open space. Voters, principally at the local level, passed 734 bills worth $26.2 billion between 1998 and 2004. Coastal communities are more likely than noncoastal communities to pass legislation to increase taxes to purchase open space, perhaps because the rapid growth in coastal areas has led to concerns about ecosystem health.[13]

If land is very expensive or if the area is large, costs may be more than government can afford. An alternative to government purchase would be land purchase by private organizations. Nongovernmental agencies such as the Nature Conservancy, the Trust for Public Land, the Land Trust Alliance, the Land Trust Exchange, and the Heritage Land Trust have preserved many valuable habitat areas by purchasing property. More than one thousand land-trust organizations throughout the nation hold or purchase donated land and easements.[14]

There is, of course, another policy change that could help protect coastal resources, and that is to curtail government subsidies that encourage costly development. Limiting public policies that encourage coastal development could lessen the costs to taxpayers created by people moving to the shore. The government programs that provide funds for flood insurance, beach nourishment, and disaster relief, for example, reduce the cost of building in hazardous areas. Although some people will choose to live in disaster-prone areas despite the personal cost, we can at least make sure that property owners bear the costs of choosing to live in hazardous areas such as the beachfront on a barrier island. Removing government subsidies may mean that as erosion threatens or storms damage property, some owners will have to abandon or relocate houses. However, taxpayers should not be picking up the tab for costs resulting from an individual's choice to live in an unstable area.

In order to move toward internalizing the cost of coastal risk, a gradual phaseout of government subsidies would be necessary. A property buyout program, such as the 1988 Stafford Act, which provided federal dollars to purchase flood-plain property, may facilitate reform. The program was used extensively following floods in 1993 in the Midwest and after the 1997 floods in the Dakotas and Minnesota.[15] If such bailouts are provided, the condemned property must not be developed again; otherwise the program would be self-defeating. New residents building in high-risk areas would pay higher prices, which grandfathers in older residents. If costs such as property insurance become too much of a burden for low-income families living in hazardous areas, a voucher similar to food stamps rather than subsidized insurance could provide assistance, but only for grandfathered residents. This would be fairer in one sense in that new people moving in would know the costs and risks of living in hazard-prone areas beforehand. Those who could not afford the higher prices in coastal areas would locate elsewhere.

All agree that the NFIP needs substantial revision. Changing the current insurance system to one with rates based on risk can help to curtail natural disaster costs for taxpayers. Kunreuther suggests that a reorganized and comprehensive national disaster insurance program that covers all natural hazards (for example earthquakes, hurricanes, and floods) may better serve the nation. Such a program would provide a greater premium base and reduce the variance associated with insurers' losses. Policyholders would benefit because insurance would cover all losses from wind and water damage. Rates should be risk-based and include incentives to discourage development in hazard-prone areas. "Long-term" insurance, which would last as long as a mortgage and have market-determined rates, may be another option to help protect home owners.[16]

In addition insurance rates should reflect the risk of erosion-related damage. A recent study recommended that the Federal Emergency Management Agency should include the cost of expected erosion losses when setting coastal flood insurance rates. Despite facing higher risk, home owners in erosion-prone areas are paying the same amount for flood insurance as are policyholders in noneroding areas. Therefore the choices of some are likely to be costly to others.[17]

In places with expensive coastal real estate, such as the Outer Banks, property owners may choose to expend significant amounts of money to protect property from storms and other threats. However, those individuals who own property on or near the beach should bear a large amount of the cost of property protection because they receive a large amount of the benefits from such measures. Removing federal subsidies to coastal development would be more equitable, more efficient, and help protect valuable resources.

In addition to implementing policies that regulate coastal development and purchasing areas to limit development, government can provide information about the risks of building in hazardous areas that may lead to improved decision making. For example, the government can provide additional information about flood hazards, flood insurance, and how to reduce flood damage. FEMA's Community Rating System encourages communities to provide such information by offering discounted premiums on flood insurance. Such information, which should encourage residents to construct houses in ways that mitigate surge damage, could be tied to an understanding that large-scale government disaster assistance for storms such as Katrina will not be available if residents choose to build in high-hazard areas. Explaining the rationale and avoiding subsidies that encourage poor decisions would be important elements of the program.

Government could disseminate additional information about the physical vulnerability of areas that could be utilized for development planning. Federal agencies such as the United States Geological Service, the Federal Emergency Management Agency, and the United States Army Corps of Engineers have identified hazard-prone shorelines based on prestorm geomorphic factors. Thieler and Hammar-Klose have created a physical vulnerability index for U.S. coastal areas based on six variables. According to this index, the highest-vulnerability areas are high-energy coastlines, generally, where the regional coastal slope is low and where the major land-form type is a barrier island. Their index shows that sections of the mid-Atlantic coast—from Maryland south to North Carolina and northern Florida—are some of the most vulnerable areas to sea-level rise.[18] The Outer Banks from Cape Hatteras north to the Virginia border is at very high risk from wave height, due in part to the orientation of the shoreline.

Given the problems that envelop densely developed coastal areas, a concentrated effort is necessary to provide a desirable outcome. Cicin-Sain and Knecht and others have suggested that integrated coastal management (ICM), which emphasizes the interrelationship between inland areas, coast, and ocean, is necessary to protect coastal areas. ICM requires interdisciplinary, intergovernmental, and international cooperation on policy solutions. The goal is to maximize the benefits of the coastal zone while minimizing the deleterious effects of resource use. Public and private decision makers should all be included in the process.

Protecting Coastal Communities from Nature's Threats

Major storms, such as hurricanes and northeasters, that regularly strike coastal areas create flooding, beach erosion, and property damage. Storms are most likely to damage properties near the ocean, which are usually the most desirable sites to build in coastal areas. In addition storms are more likely to strike some areas than others. The greatest likelihood of severe damage from hurricanes is along the coastlines of the southeastern Atlantic and Gulf of Mexico states, where 112 major hurricanes have struck between

1851 and 2006.[19] Although predictions of where the next major storm will hit are problematic, clearly some locations are more prone to suffer from storms than are others. Historically 39 percent of all major hurricanes in the United States have battered Florida, and 71 percent of Category 4 or 5 hurricane strikes have pummeled either Florida or Texas.

Several strategies will help communities withstand the threats from natural hazards. Strengthening the buildings and infrastructure that remain near the shoreline significantly improves hurricane-resistant housing. Fronstin and Holtman found that Hurricane Andrew, which struck Florida in 1992, caused less damage in subdivisions with higher average home prices. Although houses were more expensive in higher-income areas, because those houses were more storm-resistant, nearby houses suffered less damage from windblown debris. When it was instituted in 1965, the North Carolina code for hurricane-resistant buildings (the second oldest in the country) caused a major shift in coastal housing design. Among other things the code required buildings closer than 150 feet to the ocean to be erected on pilings, which raised the first floor above expected flood elevations. Property owners began to build houses 8 feet above grade (a few feet higher than minimum standards) and used the spaces under the houses for parking and storage.[20] Building codes that require such protective construction can make building and infrastructure more resistant to storm damage.

Although building codes have not always been enforced, many southeastern state and county governments are improving building standards in coastal areas. Houses in many areas must meet the wind and flood provisions of the International Building and Residential Codes that require homes built along the coast to withstand winds of 130 to 150 mph. In order to meet this standard, builders will rely more heavily on steel and concrete in construction. Construction practices such as hurricane-resistant windows, metal strapping from the foundation to the roof, and houses wrapped with plywood will become commonplace.[21] Impact-resistant windows and floors, shutters, more concrete in the foundation, stronger roof fasteners, and wind-resistant shingles all allow homes to resist hurricane damage better. However, such precautions add cost to construction.

Natural-disaster preparedness will minimize the losses caused by natural disasters. Such programs would include promoting public awareness, building hazard concerns into land-use policies, and conducting a community risk analysis. New technology such as the global positioning system will ensure better postdisaster response. Policies to mitigate costs of weather-related hazards will help decrease the damage to coastal developments.

Laws protect vegetation that stabilizes dunes, helping to
protect communities from storm damage.

Policies that protect a barrier island's natural defenses, such as building sand dunes that buffer storm surge, will help protect buildings and
infrastructure. As illustrated by Hurricane Isabel in 2003, high and wide
prestorm dunes provide some of the best protection for buildings.[22] In
addition communities should protect wetlands and floodplains, which help
buffer erosion and absorb floodwaters. Implementing land-use policies that
balance development and ecosystem protection will lessen coastal community vulnerability to storm damage. Ecosystem management, such as
protection of wetlands, which absorb some of a hurricane's impact, can
reduce storm damage. Costanza and Farber have estimated that coastal
Louisiana wetlands provided $274/acre/year (in 2008 dollars) in storm-
reduction benefits.[23] Although the Mississippi deltaic plain bordering
Louisiana provides valuable storm-damage reduction benefits, numerous
human activities have destroyed large areas of the coastal marshes. Since
1900 about 4,900 km² of wetlands in coastal Louisiana have been lost at
rates as high as 100 km²/year.

However, shore-line erosion is a continuing problem even if the natural defenses of a barrier island are protected; this is because beaches erode

and barrier islands migrate. There are three choices for coastal residents faced with disappearing sand: retreat, renourish, or armor. Retreating from eroding shorelines was generally the preferred choice until recent decades. Indeed, Bankers, who understood the impermanence of sand, built the first ocean-front houses of salvage timber and made them movable. The wisdom of this approach is apparent in South Nags Head, where the houses now in row one were in row three a mere twenty-five years ago. In a nearby motel unit three became ocean-front when storms destroyed units one and two.[24] Although Bankers are still permitted to move houses, with so much expensive property crowding the beach today there are few vacant places nearby to which the buildings could be moved. Now that the relatively sparse, cottage-style development has been replaced with multifamily behemoths crowded together, retreat will be less palatable.

However, as of 1993 in North Carolina new development permits for ocean-front structures require owners to move or dismantle buildings that are less than twenty feet from the line of stable dune vegetation nearest the sea. The Upton-Jones Amendments of the NFIP denied federal flood insurance to homes that were about to collapse into the sea because of erosion and authorized subsidies for the removal of these homes to other locations. The amendment led to the removal of 178 buildings in three years in North Carolina before it was repealed in 1994.[25]

Titus, who believes that retreat is the best solution to shore-line erosion, recommends a system of rolling easements to create an orderly retreat. Rolling easements allow development but prohibit property owners from building bulkheads or other structures that interfere with migrating shores. The low cost of rolling easements allows government to bypass the takings issue by simply purchasing the easements from current landowners. The option is also available to developers and conservancy groups and may be feasible even in areas that are already developed.[26]

The authors of a 2008 study suggest innovative solutions that will allow Outer Banks communities to adapt to changing conditions to which the barrier islands are subject.[27] Coastal highways and the constructed dune ridges would be abandoned on the Outer Banks, which would allow a "string of pearls" such as Ocracoke to develop. The eight Ocracoke-style destination villages would flourish amid more inlets and shoals and create many economic opportunities built around ecotourism.

Some believe that retreat may be the best way to save beaches. However, because many would not find retreat palatable, let us consider two alternatives—soft and hard engineering solutions—that may allow buildings to remain for a while.

Rows of sand fences such as these along the Nags
Head shoreline trap sand and build dunes.

Using a bulldozer to pile sand in front of this Nags Head
ocean-front motel is a short-term solution at best.

Beach nourishment, which is referred to as "soft stabilization," adds sand to an eroding beach. Sand is pumped from offshore or trucked from inland sources. The principal drawbacks to beach nourishment are that it is expensive and temporary. The average cost for a cubic yard of sand is approximately $5. Developed states that choose to nourish beaches should expect to spend $6 million per mile of shoreline each decade. For North Carolina this would be $690 million per decade.[28] Nourishment costs are reoccurring because sand moves—sometimes very quickly. In 1992, for example, a northeaster washed away most of the sand from a 1980s $51.2 million Ocean City, Maryland, project that nourished a nine-mile stretch of beach.

Beach-nourishment projects may damage shore-line ecosystems. Although there is much uncertainty about the biological impacts, beach-nourishment projects can alter critical habitats for nesting sea turtles and birds, bury shallow reefs, and degrade other beach habitats. In addition dredging sand offshore can modify sea-floor habitats and sedimentary character, bury plants and organisms, and block light from the water.

However, beach nourishment may make good economic sense when high-value properties are threatened.[29] On Seabrook Island, South Carolina, which is not eligible for government funding because the beaches are not open to the public, property owners have approved several beach-protection projects. On Seabrook, which suffers significant beach erosion, the community has paid millions of dollars to relocate an inlet twice and to fund several beach-nourishment projects over the past two decades. The community rejected one beach-nourishment proposal when a majority of property owners determined that the benefits of the project were less than the costs. If the government paid for most of the nourishment cost, it is likely that property owners would have approved the project.

Wider beaches produce recreational and storm-protection benefits for private home owners, many of whom may have built in precarious locations.[30] Studies show that property owners near the shoreline enjoy significant monetary benefits from beach nourishment and pay only a small portion of the costs. A beach-nourishment project completed by the ACE on South Carolina's Grand Strand, for example, added $27,410 and $41,246 of value respectively to the average ocean-front homes at Surfside Beach and Garden City.[31]

Thus an important question to consider is who should pay for beach nourishment? The federal government pays 65 percent of most Army Corps of Engineers projects as defined in the 1986 Water Resource Development Act. State and local governments share the remaining costs, with the state usually paying a larger percentage. Although the local population contributes some payment in the form of property taxes, clearly they are receiving the majority of the benefits. Rather than have farmers from Kansas paying for the beach nourishment, a more equitable system would have the principal beneficiaries pay most of the cost. Nonetheless the federal government continues to fund beach-nourishment projects, although funding has been curtailed. A planned federal project that would add 8.04 million cubic yards of sand to the Nags Head beach at a cost of $48.9 million would nourish fifteen miles of shoreline along Nags Head. For a number of years the town of Nags Head has been considering a $24 million locally funded beach-restoration plan that would add 4 million cubic yards of sand to ten miles of the town's shoreline.[32]

The third option in the crusade against shore-line erosion is to armor the shore with so-called "hard devices" such as seawalls, sandbags, and revetments. A fair amount of history teaches us about the effectiveness of hard devices such as seawalls for controlling erosion. The first attempt at erosion control in the United States was at Fort Moultrie, South Carolina, in 1829. The Army Corps of Engineers built breakwaters and jetties to prevent the walls of Fort Moultrie from slipping into the sea. The project accomplished its immediate goal. Indeed thirty-two years later Fort Moultrie, its armaments in place, took part in the bombardment of nearby Fort Sumter as the War between the States began.[33]

Property owners' efforts to protect their investments from the effects of nature's forces with hard devices are understandable. Unfortunately the barriers to the sea often destroy the very land that is so valued. A wave that runs up a natural beach expends its energy as it travels and has little energy left to carry sand back out to sea. However, when a wave strikes a seawall, much of its energy remains to carry back much of the sand. Additionally wave energy, which is concentrated on the artificial barrier, leads to increased wave scour and a steeper shore profile. The waves scour the base of the seawall, and eventually the seawall fails.[34] Even if hard devices such as jetties and seawalls provide short-term property protection, they create problems elsewhere. They rob sand from adjacent properties, thus creating erosion in other places. For the above reasons most states now prohibit permanent seawalls and other hard devices. North Carolina passed the 2003 Living Shorelines Bill, which prohibits constructing hardened structures such as seawalls and groins in ocean and inlet hazard areas. However, as illustrated by a bill that passed the North Carolina Senate in 2009 and allows groins, some interests believe that hard stabilization is desirable.

The North Carolina Division of Coastal Management may allow *temporary* construction of sandbags or artificially built dunes to allow time to move a building. Such temporary measures require permits, and a sand-bag structure must be removed within two years and may be constructed only once per ocean-front lot. However, some of the "temporary" sandbags have been on the beach for more than twenty years and have resulted in beach loss. Many of these long-lived sandbags are on the Outer Banks.[35]

The ban on armoring was upheld in a recent court case involving the Shell Island Resort located at Wrightsville Beach. When developers built the resort in the 1980s near a hazardous inlet, they understood that they would not be permitted to build a seawall. When Hurricane Fran moved the inlet dangerously close to the building, the Coastal Resources Commission (CRC) reversed itself and approved a "temporary" revetment of two-ton sandbags. After the CRC refused Shell Island's request to build a permanent seawall, the home owners sued, claiming that a "taking" of their property had occurred. The North Carolina Court of Appeals unanimously upheld the state ban on seawalls in July 1999.[36]

Other engineering techniques, such as those constructed by the Dutch and British to protect against North Sea storm surge, have been success-ful.[37] Great Britain built steel barriers across the Thames River in 1983 at a cost of £500 million to protect London from storm surge. The Dutch constructed the Oosterschelderkering, a huge barrier completed more than two decades ago, at a cost of €2.5 billion, south of Rotterdam. Such engi-neering methods may not be practical for the southeastern U.S. coastline, however, and in light of the failures of levies meant to protect New Orleans, overreliance on these measures may not be warranted. In addition struc-tural methods may provide a false sense of safety (as in New Orleans) and encourage more development in hazard-prone areas, which would increase damage costs.

The American Society of Civil Engineers (ASCE) produced a sober-ing study of engineering and planning failures that caused much of the disaster that decimated New Orleans following Katrina. The ASCE report documents many errors for which the government-sponsored engineering projects in New Orleans were responsible.[38] Two engineering failures (which were avoidable) were responsible for the levee breaches there. Poor design caused the levee flood walls (referred to as I-walls) to collapse and water to "overtop" (that is, pour over the top of) the levees. The I-walls col-lapsed because engineers failed to account for the soft soils beneath the levees; as the water filled the gap, the I-walls bowed outward and collapsed. The water overtopped the levees because engineers did not armor the levees—some of which were constructed of highly erodible soil—against erosion. The floodwaters easily scoured away the levees and poured into New Orleans. In addition the existing pump stations, which should have removed the water during and after the storm, were inoperable. The ASCE report documents other planning failures made over many years and at many levels of government.

The Outer Banks dune-stabilization project of the 1930s may be an additional example of such planning failures and overreliance on engineering methods. Indeed there is a parallel between the engineering projects on the Outer Banks and New Orleans; in both cases engineering techniques encouraged development of hazardous areas. Although the Outer Banks has not suffered Katrina's catastrophic outcome, there have been numerous dune washouts, much road damage, and many attempts to shore up the "stabilized" dunes, including beach nourishment.

Policies to Slow Climate Change

Although slowing climate change will be costly, the benefits of mitigating its effects will be substantial—especially for coastal communities. Recognizing the threats to North Carolina residents, in August 2005 the state legislature passed the North Carolina Global Warming / Climate Change Act.[39] The act created a legislative commission to study issues related to climate change and to determine if North Carolina should establish a goal to reduce pollutants that contribute to climate change. The thirty-four-member Global Warming Commission began meeting in February 2006. In 2007 the commission recommended fifty-six policy proposals to limit climate change, including a cap-and-trade program for CO_2 emissions, a surcharge for high-emission vehicles, a California-style vehicle emissions standard, and mandates for utility companies to spend money on energy-efficiency and demand-management programs.[40]

If expectations are correct that climate change will increase hurricane intensity, occurrence, and land-fall frequency, curbing the actions that contribute to climate change will be doubly important for many coastal residents. Policies to combat climate change must be considered carefully because the costs of controlling activities that contribute to climate change will be high. The bipartisan Alliance for Climate Protection, with Al Gore as chair, offers numerous policies such as improving the national electricity grid and energy efficiency. In addition investing in renewable solar, wind, and geothermal energy and carbon-sequestered coal technologies will help slow climate change.

Market-incentive policies offer the best hopes of success for a problem such as climate change. Two such policies that reduce carbon dioxide emissions—marketable permits and a carbon tax—offer promise. Marketable permits (often referred to as a "cap and trade" program), which set a limit on allowable carbon emissions, restrict greenhouse emissions in a cost-effective manner by allowing trades between polluters. For example, regulators place a "cap" or limit on the amount of carbon emissions that an emitter could produce. If an emitter is unable to limit emissions to the allowable amount, permits could be "traded" from those who have reduced emissions below the allowable amount and have credits to sell. The European Union (EU) established the first carbon-trading market in 2005, and although there have been some problems, the EU's Emission Trading System provides a valuable model. In May 2009 a U.S. House committee passed what would be the first cap-and-trade policy on industrial carbon emissions.

A carbon tax is a fee levied on carbon emissions in order to encourage polluters to decrease their emissions. An increase in the federal tax on gasoline, for example, would reduce the number of automobile miles driven and thus the amount of gasoline burned. The carbon tax could be a "green tax"; that is, policy makers could offset the gasoline tax with a decrease in payroll taxes. Therefore the tax would discourage the burning of fossil fuels but be revenue neutral and not decrease household income for most citizens. Both incentive programs encourage least-cost solutions preferable to a command-and-control policy that would dictate to emitters *how* to decrease emissions.

Policies that encourage the protection and planting of forests, which absorb carbon dioxide, will help reduce carbon dioxide emissions. Credit payments to countries that protect forests would help offset the damage from greenhouse gases. In addition policies that encourage energy efficiency, such as energy-efficient buildings, will decrease fossil fuel use. Insurance companies could encourage owners to build or rebuild to meet "green construction" standards, such as Leadership in Energy and Environmental Design standards, by discounting insurance premiums. A technology championed by the Federation of American Scientists, for example, Cementitious Structurally Insulated Panels, has wind-resistant cladding and Styrofoam cores that provide high energy efficiency and reduce the amount of wood required for construction.[41]

Protecting Coastal Resources

Communities will not benefit much from wider beaches if the beach and sea are polluted. Polluted coastal waterways have become a major problem. Businesses invest a great deal of time and effort to produce goods and services in hopes of making a profit. Firms make more profit (and consumers receive lower prices) if production costs are kept low. One way companies can keep costs lower is by dumping untreated waste into common-owned areas, such as the waterways and air. However, when such actions pollute land, water, and air, society bears the cost. Government intervention is required in order to limit this damage from pollution.

A prime governmental policy goal should be to encourage those responsible for environmental damage to pay for the costs that are being forced onto society. A secondary but important goal is to minimize the control costs. To control environmental pollution and degradation, government agencies have several policy choices, although each falls into one of two categories—command and control or market incentive. The command-and-control approach dictates the type of action that a polluter must take. For example, the government can require a utility to install a smokestack scrubber to decrease air pollution.

A market-incentive mechanism, such as an effluent fee, gives a firm more flexibility while still controlling pollution. Under the effluent-fee approach, the government gives a firm a choice: pay a fee for each unit of pollution it creates or control the pollution. The firm will try to reduce pollution emissions in order to avoid the fee. Contrary to the commonly held view that market incentives allow firms to pollute, companies will choose to clean up pollution as long as the clean-up cost is less than the fee. If society feels that the company pollutes too much at the current fee, government can increase the fee in order to encourage the firm to control more pollution. While both the command-and-control and market-incentive approaches will reduce pollution, the market approach allows firms to minimize control costs. This approach harnesses powerful market forces to encourage firms to internalize pollution costs that would otherwise be dumped on society.

The North Carolina state government has made effective use of the market-incentive approach to clean up the waterways that empty into the Outer Banks sounds. Some sources of water pollution are easier to control than others. Often government regulation can control water pollution easily if one source, such as a manufacturing plant (known as a point-source polluter), is damaging the "commons." Fine an industrial polluter or enforce effluent controls, and the polluters will reduce emissions. However, when many sources are creating the polluting, such as runoff from roadways or farms, solving the problem is much more difficult. Such non-point-source pollution is an especially difficult problem because no one polluter is responsible. The North Carolina government created an innovative market-incentive program to control the non-point-source water pollution in Pamlico Sound.

In the 1980s non-point-source pollution became a serious problem on the Tar and Pamlico rivers, which feed into Pamlico Sound. In 1983 heavy discharges of nutrients such as phosphates and nitrates caused a severe fish kill in Pamlico Sound. Some of the pollution came from the twenty-six firms (mostly publicly owned sewage-treatment plants) that were discharging waste into the two rivers within legal limits. However, non-point-source pollution from farms, dairies, and timber operations created 80 percent of the pollution. To solve the problem state officials, after setting the maximum allowable amount of nutrients to be discharged into the river, created the Tar-Pamlico River Association to manage the waterways. The not-for-profit association, formed in 1989, comprises representatives of twenty-six firms that discharge into the river system. The association charges fees for nutrient discharge and uses the revenues to pay farmers to improve their land-management practices, thus improving water quality. The market-incentive approach has successfully cleaned up the river at an annual cost of $10 million rather than the $50 to $100 million cost of the command-and-control method.[42]

In order to manage the many pressures from development, lawmakers have introduced other innovative policies. The North Carolina General Assembly established the Clean Water Management Trust Fund (CWMTF) in 1996 to issue grants to local governments, state agencies, and conservation nonprofits to help finance projects that specifically address water-pollution problems. For example, the CWMTF implemented a program to restore water quality, habitat, and buffers and to remove hog-farm lagoons from the Edenton Bay area. This first integrated fisheries restoration effort in the state was directed at a spawning and nursery area for river herring. The project included conservation easements (which are voluntary agreements between landowners and government to protect land in perpetuity) that will protect wetlands.

The CWMTF, which is a voluntary, incentive-based water-quality program, has contributed toward the protection of more than 435,573 acres and 4,560 miles of riparian buffers. Types of projects that receive funding include acquisition of buffers, floodplains, wetlands, and greenways; restoration of wetlands, riparian buffers, and streams; and storm-water management. Between 1996 and 2008 the board of trustees approved 1,148 grants for a total of $832.7 million to improve water quality, protect unpolluted waters, and create a network of riparian buffers and greenways. The grants have leveraged $1.4 billion in private and other public funds.[43]

The North Carolina Department of Marine Fisheries has numerous policies that improve water-pollution control, such as modifying statutes to prohibit ocean wastewater discharges, phasing out large-scale animal operations in sensitive areas, and expanding CAMA areas of environmental concern upstream and landward.[44] Although command-and-control legislation can be effective, governments are increasingly turning to market incentives in order to manage environmental problems. Market-incentive policies clean up just as much pollution as other policy options do but at a lower cost, while encouraging technological innovation.[45] The Farm Bill Conservation Program, for example, pays farmers to reduce their use of nitrogen, which is a major contributor to non-point-source water pollution. Changing incentive structures by paying farmers to achieve an improved environmental outcome may protect waterways more effectively. Programs that pay developers to protect coastal ecosystems may be productive as well.

Governmental policies to protect environmental resources are not always necessary. Private firms will protect the environment when they find it profitable. When developers construct residential housing, they will choose to protect environmental resources if buyers are willing to pay higher prices for environmental protection. Coastal areas are likely choices for developers to protect because increasing numbers of affluent people who desire natural areas are moving to these locations.

Dewees Island, South Carolina, is an excellent example of developers protecting a community's environment because they felt that buyers would value a "green'" community. The island, once a hideaway for pirates, is located a few miles north of Charleston. In 1991 an investment group— Island Partner Partnership—began developing Dewees Island with the intent of protecting the environment. The developers worked with local and regional environmental groups to ensure that the development minimized energy and water use as well as waste and habitat disturbance. The restrictions that planners implemented to protect the natural environment include the following: no automobiles are permitted on the island; no concrete or asphalt is allowed; only plants and trees native to the island can be used for landscaping; and only organic pesticides are permitted. Erosion and runoff are reduced, and the aquifer is recharged sooner because impervious surfaces are prohibited. Strict regulations, such as requiring houses to be built well back from the beach, are in place to protect the dunes, vegetation, creeks, lakes, and wetlands.[46]

Only 150 houses will be built on the twelve-hundred-acre island, and each house is restricted to a seventy-five-hundred-square-foot disturbance area. Buyers willingly pay the highest prices in the area for the properties because they value the natural environment. The goal is to leave 90 percent of the island undisturbed; 65 percent has been designated a wildlife refuge and will never be disturbed. As of 2008, 62 houses had been built on Dewees and 3 more were under construction. Developers have gone to great lengths to protect the environment in many other communities, such as Seaside, Florida, and Kiawah Island, South Carolina. The communities have strict covenants that residents agree to when locating in the areas; the legal agreements ensure future protection of the ecosystem.

Protecting Fisheries

As is the case with many other ocean fisheries around the world, those along the Outer Banks are being overused. Overharvesting is the principal cause, although factors such as water pollution, habitat loss, and reef damage contribute to the problem of fish-stock depletion. Part of the solution is to protect habitat areas from damage and to restore habitats, such as wetlands. However, solving the "tragedy of the commons," which explains that a resource tends to be overused when demand for said resource is high and no single agent limits access, is the most important goal. Changing incentive structure is the key to fishery protection. When no one owns the fish, each fisher catches as many fish as possible because what he or she does not catch will be caught by someone else. No one has an incentive not to overfish. However, an owner of a catfish farm would not overfish his/her farm because he/she knows that this means less profit in the end.

To stop overharvesting of fisheries, an agent, often government, must control access and limit the amount of fish that are caught. One way government can limit catch is to make fishers less efficient, which was a solution imposed on oyster harvesters along the Outer Banks in 1900. The state government allowed dredging for oysters by sail only, which caused the fishers to work harder but to catch fewer oysters. Although the policy of "regulated inefficiency" decreased the number of oysters harvested, it increased the cost of catching the oysters.

A better solution than regulated inefficiency is to control access by a rights-based fishing system, which fishery managers have developed over the past twenty-five years. With the rights-based system officials determine the sustainable yield for a fishery and issue a limited number of permits to an individual fisher, community, or other entity to catch a specified portion of the total allowable catch. One type of rights-based system, an individual transferable quota (ITQ), allows a fisher to transfer or sell a quota right to other fishers. A cooperative, which splits all or part of the available quota among various fishing and processing entities within a fishery, is another rights-based system variation.

A rights-based system limits the number of fish that are caught and ensures that the best quality fish are caught at the lowest possible cost because the most efficient fishers will purchase the permits. By ending the race for fish, anglers can fish more safely as well as minimize gear loss and bycatch of protected and other nontargeted species. Fishers can develop better long-range business plans because they can more accurately anticipate their annual catches and are less likely to overinvest in boats and gear. Consumers benefit because fresh, rather than frozen, fish are available most of the year. In addition the rights-based system improves fishery regulatory policy, which can be controversial and difficult to enforce. Fishers, who have a financial stake in sustainable practices, are more easily convinced to make sacrifices required to rebuild and sustain fisheries. The U.S. Coast Guard will not be overwhelmed by thousands of fishers operating in small areas or during a compressed season.

Currently seven U.S. fisheries grant some form of rights-based system: the surf-clam/ocean-quahog fishery in the mid-Atlantic (ITQ); the wreckfish fishery in the South Atlantic (ITQ); the halibut/sablefish fishery in the North Pacific (ITQ); the Pacific whiting fishery (co-op); the Bering Sea pollock fishery in the North Pacific (co-op); Alaska's Community Development Quota program (community quota); and the Chignik salmon fishery (co-op). Many other countries, including New Zealand, Australia, and Iceland, rely heavily on rights-based systems for fishery management.[47]

Recognizing the desirability of a rights-based policy, a federal panel created by President George W. Bush in December 2004 plans to expand such programs. The committee, headed by James Connaughton (chair of the White House Council on Environmental Quality), was created in response to the gloomy assessment of the U.S. Commission on Ocean Policy's 2003 report. The committee, which is to coordinate oceanic policy, will attempt to win ratification of the Law of the Sea, an international regulatory system governing fishing, navigation, and other oceanic issues.[48]

The conflict between commercial and recreational users of fisheries will continue to require policy makers' attention. Given the fact that recreational fishers generate more revenue for the local economy, it is likely that commercial fishers will continue to be squeezed. Aquaculture production, which is the business of fish farming, is a growing industry that is replacing many commercial fishers. Aquaculture works well with fish that are not very mobile, such as oysters, tilapia, and catfish. In 1970 about 4 percent of fish consumed globally were farm raised, and by 2000 farm-raised fish composed more than 27 percent of the market. Projections are that by 2050, 50 percent of aquatic foods will come from aquaculture.

In 1948, as the cold war was heating up, the U.S. government decided to move nuclear weapons testing from the Marshall Islands to a place somewhere in the United States. Although the location needed to meet a number of criteria, primarily the site had to be expendable because the radiation from the tests would make the area uninhabitable. In a top-secret study, code-named Nutmeg, the Atomic Energy Commission found that "several areas are suitable for test sites between Cape Hatteras and Cape Lookout." Possible sites included Cape Hatteras, Ocracoke, and Portsmouth. The Outer Banks was a desirable test site because "population is not dense, meteorology is favorable during two-thirds of the year between 20% and 30% of the time; and the waters of the Gulf Stream will remove the waste products to the open Atlantic." Ultimately the Atomic Energy Commission chose Nevada for weapons testing, and the Outer Banks was spared.[49]

The Outer Banks is held in much higher regard today. Not only does the government no longer consider exploding nuclear bombs there, but also considerable resources are expended to protect the islands. Federal, state, and local governments undertake policies to help limit the damage created by population growth, for example. The challenge is to find the most efficient methods to protect the Outer Banks from the inadvertent damage that humans cause. We can have cleaner water, protect wilderness areas, and preserve historical places but only at a cost. However, protecting the natural environment is good economic policy because people value and are willing to pay for environmental amenities such as beautiful beaches. Indeed protecting natural landscapes, which enhance property values, may be the best way to protect the long-run economic vitality of the Outer Banks.

Seven

Time and Chance

But time and chance happenth to them all.

Ecclesiastes 9:11

. . . .

Often communities develop at specific locations because some natural features promote commerce. Port cities, for example, develop in locations that
offer ships deepwater harbors and shelter from storms. The first major cities
in the United States were port cities—such as New York, Charleston, and
New Orleans   that prospered because of the shipping trade. Many other
types of natural features have contributed to the development of towns. In
the 1800s owners of manufacturing plants located their factories near rivers
with large falls in order to use the power generated by the moving water.
The mechanized cotton textile industry located near swift rivers in towns
such as Waltham, Patterson, and Roxbourough rather than in the nearby
cities of Boston, New York, and Philadelphia. Other towns, such as Oil
City, Pennsylvania (the location of the first U.S. oil well), developed when
prospectors discovered valuable resources.

Sometimes, however, the natural feature that was the impetus for a
town's birth is exhausted, and the community expires along with its purpose for being. Towns with colorful names such as High Lonesome, New
Mexico; Silver City, Nevada; and Rough and Ready, Arizona, thrived for a
time but are now "Old West" ghost towns. Many western towns that flourished for only a short time had a similar history. They would spring up
overnight in remote locations when prospectors discovered valued minerals. Entrepreneurs would rush in and start up saloons, hardware stores,
hotels, and other businesses to meet the needs of the miners. Then when
the gold or silver played out, people had little reason to stay, and these
boomtowns withered away. Today the places are mostly or completely de-
serted, with only a few neglected buildings remaining to remind the curious visitor that the Fates are not always kind to a community.

Although when one thinks of ghost towns, one usually thinks of the
colorful, Wild West, ghost towns can be found elsewhere. A fine example

of a ghost town exists on Portsmouth Island. The town of Portsmouth, which was for many years the most populated town on the Outer Banks, has quite a different story from that of the typical Old West ghost town, although natural features created Portsmouth, just as natural features created Old West towns.

Portsmouth's history illustrates the vagaries of life on a barrier island and how the environment, natural events, and chance shape the destiny of a community there. A barrier island along the Atlantic or Gulf coastline can be a precarious place to build a community, especially with the threat of hurricanes and northeasters. Indeed, some coastal scientists and planners warn of catastrophic storms that will eventually strike the towns on barrier islands and consequently make these areas unlivable. The strong winds and ocean floodwaters that accompany the most damaging storms have been known to destroy whole towns, and it would not be surprising if storms had driven off the inhabitants of Portsmouth. However, the events that led to the decline of Portsmouth are more complex and surprising.

The Settlement of Portsmouth

Portsmouth Island is shaped like a seven-mile-long chicken drumstick. The northern end of the island, which is more than two miles wide, is the thick part of the drumstick. As the island stretches toward the southwest, it narrows to one mile. It is oriented northeast to southwest, which is almost parallel to the prevailing winds. Such an orientation creates low-lying land with poorly developed dune fields and sparse vegetation, which allow frequent ocean overwash. Salt- and freshwater marshes cover the island, which supports a maritime forest of cedars, yaupons, and myrtle bushes. A unique feature of the island is an extensive area of sand flats, which are almost a mile wide and run parallel to the ocean beach for five miles. The reason for the extensive flats is unknown but may be related to the large sand supply in and around Ocracoke Inlet.

Ocracoke Inlet borders Portsmouth Island to the north, and Whalebone Inlet, which is opened only periodically, marks the southern boundary. Ocracoke Inlet, which separates Portsmouth from Ocracoke by about a mile, is the oldest existing inlet on the Outer Banks. Along the Outer Banks, where inlets frequently open or close, Ocracoke, which dates from pre-1585, is a monument to steadfastness. Raleigh's expedition sailed through the inlet and charted the area. However, the shoals and sandbars that crisscross Ocracoke Inlet shift continually, and only an expert navigator who knows the tendencies of the inlet is able to manage the difficult currents. In fact, the inlet's dangerous contours explain why Portsmouth became the first Outer Banks community.

In the early 1700s only a small number of people lived on the Outer Banks, and Portsmouth Island was no exception. The first European inhabitants to settle Portsmouth were principally Virginia renegades, shipwreck victims, and wayward sailors. The unsavory reputation of the early residents, which made Portsmouth an undesirable community for families, stunted early settlement there. Between 1713 and 1718 some of the most unsavory residents were smugglers and pirates who thrived near Ocracoke Inlet. During this short but colorful period known as the "Golden Age of Pirates," the lawbreakers depended on the treacherous inlet to escape capture and avoid paying customs duties. Piracy along the Outer Banks ended shortly after British seamen killed Blackbeard, the most celebrated brigand, at Ocracoke Inlet on November 22, 1718. After the decline of piracy, Portsmouth became a more hospitable environment for community development.

Although Portsmouth was in a favorable location to benefit from the shipping trade, it was not a deepwater port like New York or Charleston. In fact, there were no good deepwater ports for European ships to unload their cargoes anywhere along the 175 miles of the Outer Banks shoreline. The shallow waters and treacherous shoals of the inlets prevented European ships from passing through the inlets into the sounds. However, enterprising entrepreneurs devised an alternative "route" to get goods to the mainland; their practical solution was to "lighter" the large vessels. Pilots would shift the cargoes from the larger ships arriving from Europe onto smaller boats, which could navigate the inlets and carry the goods across the shallow sounds to be unloaded on the mainland. Consequently the earliest town on the Outer Banks was located at a transshipment point, which is a location where goods are transferred from one transport mode to another. Once the cargoes reached the mainland, they would then be shipped to their final destinations. Portsmouth was a favorable transshipment point because Ocracoke Inlet was the only outlet for ships transporting goods to and from ports on the Neuse, Roanoke, and Pamlico rivers.

However, because the ships would sometimes have to lie out at anchor for days before they could be lightered, the transfer to smaller boats could be treacherous; severe weather could damage the ships, and pirates could plunder them. In addition traders could use other inlets and avoid paying customs fees. Officials realized that to facilitate trade with the mainland, daily life on Portsmouth would need to be more civilized and orderly. As early as 1731 Governor George Burrington began to agitate for the establishment of a customhouse at Ocracoke Inlet. In 1736 Burrington wrote, "If a collector is settled at Ocracoke it will be difficult to bring into that part of the province any prohibited goods, without paying the King's Duty, because all vessels that come down from the rivers or sail from sea are to be seen a long time before they enter harbor."[1]

Although Portsmouth and Ocracoke islands were in a prime geographical location for development, it took a decree from the state assembly to establish a stable community on Portsmouth. In 1753 the North Carolina Assembly authorized the town of Portsmouth, named for one of Britain's great naval ports, to expedite the transportation of cargo from oceangoing ships to the colonies. Planners located the town of Portsmouth on the northern end of Portsmouth Island next to Ocracoke Inlet and on the sound side of the island in order to be as far away as possible from the force of ocean storms. The town was built around Fort Granville, which housed a small garrison of soldiers between 1758 and 1764. The fort was built to protect against Spanish attacks along the coast, which were common in the early eighteenth century. However, no battle was ever fought at Portsmouth, and following the conclusion of the French and Indian War, the garrison was removed.

With the lightering business thriving, in 1798 John Wallace of Portsmouth and John Gray Blount of Washington, North Carolina, created a lightering hub on Old Rock, a half-mile stretch of oyster beds in Ocracoke Inlet. Wallace and Blount changed the name to Shell Castle Island, which at its peak housed forty people to handle the maritime traffic. On the small island the two entrepreneurs built a thriving business, which consisted of warehouses, a dock, a gristmill, a windmill, a ship's store and chandlery, and a lighthouse. Workers unloaded ships' cargoes onto the wharves to be stored in warehouses until the cargoes could be loaded into shallow-draft boats, which then carried the goods across Pamlico Sound to the mainland.

By the end of the colonial period, thanks to lightering, Portsmouth and Ocracoke were the only significant settlements on the Outer Banks. As the nineteenth century began, the two towns were flourishing seaports with as many as fourteen hundred vessels a year using Ocracoke Inlet and carrying nearly two-thirds of North Carolina's exports. When two inlets north of Portsmouth closed—Roanoke in 1811 and Currituck in 1828—traffic at Ocracoke Inlet increased even more. Economic prosperity encouraged community development, and by the early 1800s a school, a post office, a Methodist church, and several taverns had been built on Portsmouth. Government officials established a customhouse for the District of Ocracoke in 1806 and a marine hospital (mainly for use by sick seamen) in 1846.

By 1850, 505 residents lived in Portsmouth, doubling the population from fifty years before. Ocracoke Inlet grew to become the largest seaport between Norfolk, Virginia, and Charleston, South Carolina. As the islanders neared the midpoint of the nineteenth century, more than 1,000 people were distributed evenly between Portsmouth and Ocracoke. This was more than one-third of the total Outer Banks population. Despite the inherently precarious nature of life on a barrier island, a solid community was rooted in the shifting sands of Portsmouth. Island residents might have expected continued good fortune to result from their hard work. However, daily life for the bustling town full of workers busy on the wharves and in the warehouses was about to change in a way that no reasonable Portsmouther might have expected.

The 1846 Hurricane

The word "hurricane" comes from the Spanish *huricon,* which is borrowed from the name of an evil spirit feared by the Tairo, inhabitants of the Caribbean when Europeans first arrived. It is easy to understand the fear and terror that hurricanes create since they unleash some of the most awesome power on earth. At sea hurricanes have created storm waves greater than thirty-eight feet high that have sunk great vessels with all hands on deck. On land wind and storm surge create a potent duo of destruction. Roaring winds that can exceed two hundred mph bring torrential rains and hurl deadly projectiles through the air. The terrible sounds of projectiles smashing into objects and crushing structures accompany the disastrous storms. Storm surge, which can be twenty feet high or more, is often the most dangerous element. In 1900 the storm surge that inundated Galveston, Texas, caused most of the twelve thousand deaths that occurred.

Although hurricanes are almost as much a part of the Outer Bankers' way of life as the sea air, islanders would never take an approaching storm lightly. Some of the worst hurricanes in U.S. history have collided with the Outer Banks, which juts far out into the Atlantic Ocean. The hurricane of July 12, 1842, which was one of the worst in the history of coastal North Carolina, damaged all but one building on Portsmouth, blew twenty-eight vessels aground, sank two other ships, and killed numerous livestock.[2]

With hurricanes frequently striking the Outer Banks, Portsmouth Islanders were experienced hurricane survivors who respected the life-threatening power of such storms. Islanders would take any precaution that would lessen the danger from hurricanes. None would have been foolish enough to build on the oceanfront, where one would be most susceptible to storm surge. Instead islanders built houses on the sound side as far as possible from possible ocean storm surge to minimize any damage. To prepare for extreme storms that brought the greatest storm surge, many islanders built trapdoors in the floors of their homes. These trapdoors were not to let the inhabitants out; *they were to let the water in.* If the water rose high enough, a homeowner would open the trapdoor to allow the rising water to enter the house more rapidly, thus preventing the building from floating off its foundation and drifting away.

After taking the few precautions available, islanders could only remain watchful for signs of an approaching hurricane. They hoped that the storm would not strike at night because there would be little warning and the damage could be severe. Today, with modern meteorological technology, an approaching hurricane surprises no one. We watch televised satellite images of the hurricane forming and moving across the warm tropical waters. The Weather Channel produces a round-the-clock spectacle, educating and entertaining the populace with experts before, during, and after the event, on location as well as in the studio. Television viewers map the hurricane, following the storm's progress closely from birth to landfall. Hurricanes, appropriately named and categorized, attain celebrity status—especially those that are most damaging and deadly.

However, seasoned Bankers did not need a weather channel or advanced weather-tracking technology to recognize that a major storm was approaching on the first days of September 1846. Because this was peak hurricane season, they were on the lookout for warning signs—based on their own experiences and those of generations before them—of an approaching disturbance. The first indication that a major storm was approaching was the surging ocean, which began piling up several feet of water along the coastline a day or two before the hurricane arrived. By September 4 groundswells pounded the Portsmouth Island shore, and water pushed much farther up the beach than was typical. The huge ocean swells traveling great distances ahead of the storm crashed on the shore, creating a roar heard across the island. On the 5th, as the hurricane neared, thick, dark clouds obscured the sky; the winds grew stronger, bending vegetation to the ground and whipping grains of sand into a stinging fusillade.

Even though Bankers knew a storm was approaching, they could not predict how severe it would be. In the Atlantic a hurricane's right front quadrant, which produces the highest winds and greatest tidal surge, poses the greatest threat to island residents. When a hurricane approaches the Outer Banks from the south, as many do, the right front quadrant, which is on the northeastern side of the hurricane, remains at sea. Frequently hurricanes approaching from the south only skirt the Outer Banks, leaving the most damaging elements of the storm at sea. Unfortunately for the islanders, the 1846 storm would bring the full wrath of the Tairo's evil spirit.

By the time the islanders recognized the severity of the storm, it was too late to evacuate people from the Outer Banks. The waters would be too rough for evacuation by boat, and there was no bridge to the mainland. Portsmouth Islanders prepared to ride out the storm as best they could.

They herded livestock together onto some of the higher land and lashed down or stored away lumber, tools, and other objects that could become deadly projectiles. As the hurricane approached, people huddled in the safest homes (usually those on the highest ground, which the floodwaters would reach last) and prayed for the worst of the storm to pass.

The hurricane reached the Outer Banks on September 6, bringing rain squalls that periodically lashed the island. Ocean waves soon rolled over the lower portions of the island, and the swirling water whisked objects out to sea. Before long the storm surge poured over even the highest portions of the island and began to cover the land. As the seawater began flooding and pushing homes from their foundations, people ripped open the trap-doors to let the water rush in. Some who had not built trapdoors in the floors of their homes frantically chopped holes in the floors with axes. In the midst of the hurricane the howling wind was like the Devil's breath hurling dangerous projectiles, such as snapped tree limbs, in all directions; tearing shingles from roofs; and even ripping off entire roofs. Although there were occasional periods of comparative quiet, the wind soon picked up again, banging and beating the homes. After some time, perhaps an hour, the hurricane moved inland, and residents began to survey the damage.

The 1846 storm was as destructive as a hurricane could be, perhaps worse than the 1842 storm. There is no way of knowing exactly how strong the hurricane was since prior to 1870 no actual measurements of storm winds were made. However, based on the reported storm damage, we might expect that the 1846 hurricane was a Category 4 storm with sustained winds between 131 and 155 mph. We learn from an eyewitness, Sarah Ann Clark, of some of the hurricane's damage. In a letter Clark, who was vacationing on Portsmouth during the storm, wrote, "The inhabitants say this was the hardest wind they had had in 20 years."[3] The storm surge drowned cattle, sheep, hogs, and chickens. More than a dozen boats were driven ashore on Portsmouth, and at least one schooner, the *Mary Ann*, was sunk. The storm destroyed bridges, docks, fishing equipment, boats, and homes.

Although the hurricane was past Portsmouth on September 7, it had not finished with the community yet. During the storm the winds, blow-ing from the east, forced large amounts of ocean water through the inlets and into the sounds. The winds continued to push the combined ocean and sound waters farther west into the bays and estuaries, flooding low-land areas on the mainland. The storm pushed so much water out of the sounds that one could walk across them to the mainland. Then, as the hurricane moved west of the Outer Banks, the winds shifted direction. This is usual progress for hurricanes in the Northern Hemisphere, where winds churn counterclockwise. Hurricane winds blow from the east as they approach the Outer Banks and from the west once over land. Now the water that the storm had backed up into the rivers would be forced back to the sea.

On the morning of September 7 the winds shifted onshore and began forcing the massive amount of water back toward the sea, washing over the Outer Banks from west to east. At 11:00 A.M., finding the point of least resistance, the water cut channels across low, narrow sections of the Outer Banks. C. O. Boutelle, the assistant superintendent of the U.S. Coast Survey at the time, provided an eyewitness account. Boutelle reported that a sudden squall from the southwest signaled the reversal of waters. Rushing water two to three feet high cut through the beach on Bodie Island, creating a new opening to the ocean at a place where homes were located.[4] On September 8 another river of water created a second new inlet across Hatteras Island. The water passage cutting across Bodie Island was named Oregon Inlet because that was the name of the first boat to sail through the new inlet. The second inlet, created between Old Hatteras Inlet and the village of Hatteras, was named New Hatteras Inlet.

Following the storm the residents of Portsmouth began the usual cleanup and return to daily life. As ruinous as the hurricane was, islanders who had weathered many before understood that such storms were part of life on Portsmouth. However, things were not as they seemed. The damage from this hurricane was greater and more enduring than the losses caused by previous ones, although the residents did not realize yet how the hurricane had affected all that was to follow.

Both new inlets diverted water away from Ocracoke Inlet, which began to shoal. Before long ship traffic began shifting to the new inlets, which offered better passageways. Most boat traffic switched to New Hatteras Inlet, which provided an entrance into Pamlico Sound, although some small fishing boats switched to Oregon Inlet, which provided a more direct route to the Albemarle Sound ports. Portsmouth's days as a major transshipment point clearly were numbered. As steam-powered vessels, which were able to navigate the northern inlets more easily, became more prevalent, boat traffic at Portsmouth declined further. In addition the expansion of railroads allowed more goods to be shipped by inland railroads. The town began a gradual but inevitable decline as businesses and jobs shifted elsewhere in the years following the 1846 hurricane.

Portsmouth inhabitants temporarily abandoned the town in 1861, when Union troops captured Fort Hatteras and Fort Clark on Hatteras Island. Following the Civil War and faced with poor economic prospects at Portsmouth, only about one-half of the population returned. As jobs from the maritime traffic declined, many islanders switched to fishing, principally for menhaden. In 1866 entrepreneurs built a plant that processed menhaden into oil and fertilizer. Although similar plants were thriving on New York's Long Island and Shelter Island, the plant on Portsmouth was short-lived. In 1867 Portsmouth's customhouse was moved to New Bern, and the hospital burned down in 1894. A U.S. Coast Guard lifesaving station, opened in 1895, failed to provide sufficient jobs to stem further decline, although it was a major influence in the community until it was decommissioned in 1937. The population continued to decline following a succession of damaging storms, especially one in 1899 that damaged Portsmouth more than any other island. With few job prospects, people continued drifting away. Portsmouth's population declined to 341 in 1870 and to 150 by 1900.

As the twentieth century began, with little industry to sustain communities anywhere along the Outer Banks, economic survival was difficult. The Great Depression made matters marginally worse. The infusion of government spending in the 1920s that spurred modest growth on some Outer Banks islands did not occur on Portsmouth. The changes that created the modern Outer Banks tourism-based economy never reached Portsmouth, and the community continued to decline. The schoolhouse was closed in 1943, and mail service ended in 1949. By 1950, a century after Portsmouth's peak, only fourteen people remained on the island. Then in 1971, when Henry Pigott, the last man on the island, died, Elma Dixon and Marion Gray Babb, the remaining two residents, reluctantly moved to the mainland.

Survival on the Outer Banks was always difficult, and when Portsmouth's only major industry—lightering—withered, the town was unable to adapt. Other industries, such as menhaden fishing, were unsuccessful. Without the benefit of infrastructure such as bridges and roads, Portsmouth at that time was unable to develop a tourism industry. The economy and population that had thrived for a century eroded away like the shore-line sand, until all that was left was a ghost town.

Preserving Portsmouth

In the early 1970s, with no one living on Portsmouth, the island's prospects were uncertain at best. Fortunately in 1976 Portsmouth became part of the Cape Lookout National Seashore, which about one hundred thousand people visit each year. Those who visit the 250-acre Portsmouth historic district, which is listed on the National Register of Historic Places, begin at Haulover Landing on the island's northwest corner. A sandy road winds through the town's remaining buildings, which are in various stages of repair. The National Park Service maintains some structures, such as the Dixon/Salter House, which has been converted into a visitors' center. Henry

Pigott's house is freshly painted, and you almost expect to see him rocking on his front porch. Other neglected buildings are collapsing to the sand, strangled with vines. The modest houses, which are mostly single story, indicate that this was a working-class community.

The Methodist church, destroyed by a storm in 1913 but rebuilt in 1914, is well preserved. The church is modestly and simply built but with attention to detail. People still occasionally hold weddings in the white wooden building with pointed windows and a tiered steeple. The Life Saving Service Complex, built in 1894, is in good repair, and the post office, the social hub of the community when Portsmouth flourished, still stands. Cedars, yaupons, and myrtle bushes, though stunted by salt spray, cover the land, and tall marsh grasses sway in the wind. Missing from the island, along with the inhabitants, are the cattle, pigs, and sheep that used to browse the grasses. Not missing are the mosquitoes, which during much of the year, and especially in the summer, swarm from the stagnant pools and abandoned cisterns.

After two centuries of human activity Portsmouth now stands as a ghost town, a doppelgänger to Ocracoke. Today only occasional visitors, more interested in quiet contemplation of times past than in a Nags Head all-you-can-eat buffet spot, wander Portsmouth's quiet paths. The Portsmouth visitor experiences an eerie nostalgia of a time when the town bustled with activity.

None of those five hundred residents at Portsmouth who cleaned up on the days following the 1846 storm could have realized how the hurricane had changed the community's future. Today hurricanes are much more costly, in dollar terms, than the 1846 storm was. This is because the number of people living in coastal areas has increased in recent decades and because the homes people build are much more expensive. However, the 1846 storm destroyed much more than property. The hurricane destroyed the community's means of economic survival and ultimately the community itself.

Of course Portsmouth would not have been able to survive on lightering forever. Change is inevitable, and other factors would have forced the islanders to find alternative livelihoods. By 1900 cargo ships no longer docked at any Outer Banks port. Portsmouth could never have become a major port city like Norfolk, Virginia, or Charleston, South Carolina, because of the lack of deep water. However, if the 1846 hurricane had not altered the geography of the Outer Banks as it did, the community may have been able to survive long enough to adjust to the changing economic conditions and effect a smoother transition to the twentieth century.

The communities of Portsmouth and Ocracoke both continued into the twentieth century, although by 1900, while 548 people lived in Ocracoke,

Reminders of the Portsmouth Island community, such as the
Pigott house, are maintained by the National Park Service.

Although the community of Portsmouth Island has disappeared,
the Methodist church, built in 1914, remains and is open to the public.

only 150 residents remained in Portsmouth. Today Ocracoke is a quiet community of about 700 residents that maintains many of the qualities of a small fishing village but survives on tourist dollars. Why did Ocracoke survive but Portsmouth did not? Three government-sponsored activities on Ocracoke may help provide the answer.[5]

First, the government dredged Cockle Creek and constructed Silver Lake Harbor in 1931. This provided a needed port that the fishing industry used originally but the navy used during World War II. Second, in 1952 most of Ocracoke Island became part of the Cape Hatteras National Seashore. Although some actions of the National Park Service angered some Ocracokers (such as buying property that Ocracokers had owned for generations), the government provided erosion control and the promise of tourism dollars. Third, the government completed the Ocracoke highway in 1957 and subsidized ferry service from Hatteras Island and Cedar Island to Ocracoke. This modest provision of transportation infrastructure encouraged tourists to visit Ocracoke, providing some income for the residents.

Would a tourism-based economy, encouraged by government activities, have allowed Portsmouth to survive as Ocracoke and other Outer Banks communities currently do? Most likely. However, other events transpired. Ocracoke Inlet made Portsmouth a desirable location for a port in the eighteenth and early nineteenth centuries. It was the reliance on the lightering industry that eventually caused the demise of Portsmouth, just as overreliance on a single industry led to the demise of Old West ghost towns.

With barrier islands becoming so congested, to find a ghost-town barrier island, especially along one of the fastest developing coastlines in the country, is unusual, and ironic. Today if an event similar to the 1846 hurricane would cause an inlet to shoal, how would people respond? We might expect that special-interest groups would seek government aid. The Army Corps of Engineers would dredge and stabilize Ocracoke Inlet; no *taxpayer* expense would be spared. Once the island was restored, developers might build private, gated communities with exclusive golf courses and marinas on the island, subsidized with other government programs.

Many events can cause the decline of a community. Some coastal scientists warn of widespread disaster for communities built on erosive shorelines and recommend that we prepare to abandon the shore. The cause of Portsmouth's demise was subtler and less dramatic. Portsmouth became a ghost town not because of direct storm damage but because of natural alteration and simple economics: no navigable inlet, no lightering industry, no maritime jobs. The 1846 hurricane may not have been the most damaging to hit the Outer Banks when measured in property damage or loss of life, but the changes effected by that hurricane altered the course of an entire community.

On the Outer Banks change created by nature is inevitable but impossible to predict. All that is certain is change. In addition the repercussions from change are never isolated; each alteration creates fresh reverberations. After some passage of time one can examine and interpret the interconnected series of past events and sometimes wonder at nature's irony. Such is the tale of Portsmouth. The town that was the first and for many years the most populated on the Outer Banks is today a ghost town.

The history of Portsmouth is in some ways appropriate for a barrier-island community that is so intertwined with the forces of nature. Wind and water eroded mountains, creating sediment that rivers carried to the ocean. This sediment became the sand on which Portsmouth was founded. Wind and water destroyed the reason for the Portsmouth Island community, and today one can see the remains of a once-thriving population. If the Fates had been kinder, perhaps today Portsmouth would not be a ghost town. Instead the Portsmouth one sees today provides a poignant picture much different from that of the typical island community.

Portsmouth's history is unique because, unlike in the case of Diamond City, which people abandoned after the 1899 hurricane inundated Shackleford Banks, the hurricane damage was not the direct cause of Portsmouth's demise. The gradual decline of lightering, caused by the 1846 hurricane that changed the inlets, was responsible for the decline of Portsmouth.

Because the island was not part of the 1930s dune-stabilization project, today Portsmouth must look much as it did a century ago. Seeing Portsmouth today, one can envision what life may have been like for the one hundred or so residents who remained on the island in the early decades of the twentieth century. Despite declining economic prospects, several accounts provide an idyllic picture of life for inhabitants, who lived a quiet, isolated, and simple lifestyle. Herds of free-roaming livestock browsed the vegetation, contributing to the low windswept appearance of the island. Families harvested food from the sea, maintained separate buildings for summer cooking, and, although there was no refrigeration, kept a shaded, screened dairy house where cooling sea breezes kept perishables fresh. After the post office closed in 1949, Henry Pigott, an elderly African American, would pole his skiff into the sound to meet the boat that sailed between Cedar Island and Ocracoke to exchange mail and pick up groceries for the few remaining islanders. It was, as Ben Salter reminisces, a time "when people enjoyed themselves better."[6]

Yet when the wind blows off the ocean, visitors to Portsmouth may feel that something remains from that place and time. Along with the hissing waves they may hear echoes of voices and lives from a busy and happy existence—a place and time of pleasant and cheerful tranquillity.

Eight

An Apprenticeship with Change

Whenever a thing changes and alters its nature, at that moment comes the death of what it was before.

Lucretius, 2:753 and 3:519

As the history of Portsmouth Island illustrates, the well-being of Outer Bankers is linked to the changing island environment; this is true today just as when humans first visited the islands. In addition to this connection, the landforms of the Outer Banks are valuable for many reasons. These strips of sand protect the mainland from the full brunt of hurricanes, provide important habitats for plant and animal life, and offer a place to renourish the weary human spirit. Unfortunately a combination of human and natural forces that threaten the quality of life on the Outer Banks will force today's inhabitants to make difficult choices. The history of a people, place, and time far from today's Outer Banks might provide some perspective.

In the arid southwestern United States desert one can traverse the ruins of a great, and enigmatic, Native American civilization that began, and ended, long before Europeans ever sighted the Outer Banks. Beginning about 900 C.E., generations of Anasazi, or "Ancient Ones," as the Navajo refer to them, built a complex community in western New Mexico's Chaco Canyon. The Anasazi built well-crafted four- to five-story-high masonry pueblos, which were the highest buildings in North America until the late nineteenth century when steel became available. The Anasazi used more than 215,000 wood beams to construct the buildings that contained as many as seven hundred rooms. The expansive buildings may have rivaled the pyramids in grandeur. There is evidence that the Anasazi also created an irrigation system to enhance crop production. In addition the Anasazi built hundreds of miles of carefully engineered roads that extended their influence throughout much of the Southwest.

Researchers, who have explored the ruins for the past one hundred years, have been searching for answers to many puzzling questions about the Anasazi civilization. Why did the Native Americans choose to develop a community in a barren area with limited resources and a harsh climate when there were locations that were more hospitable to develop a community? Where did the Anasazi get the wood beams used in construction? Where did they find the water in such an arid area? Although the southwestern desert environment is beautiful in its sparseness, it is not rich in the resources needed for sustenance. The desert plant and animal species—such as scrub bush, lizards, and rattlesnakes—that have adapted to the harsh environment provide little food or materials for human survival. Temperatures can be extreme in Chaco Canyon. The blazing summer sun forces temperatures as high as 110°, and biting winter winds drop temperatures well below 0°.

Inexplicably around 1200 C.E. the community that numbered in the thousands at its height abruptly disappeared, leaving behind only more puzzling questions. Why did the Anasazi abruptly leave the community that they had spent so much effort building? Did war decimate the community? Did a religious event cause a rapid departure? Answering these perplexing questions has been difficult because the Anasazi left no written records. However, researchers, making use of an unusual source, have found clues to help answer some of the questions. The surprising answers have been provided by desert rodents.

Packrats collected bits of debris and deposited them in middens or refuse mounds that have survived for centuries in Chaco Canyon caves. When paleobotanists examined these time capsules from the period when the Anasazi inhabited Chaco, they found evidence of a much more hospitable environment than the one we see today. Based on evidence from the packrats, paleobotanists believe that when the Anasazi first began their community, a pinyon-juniper woodland and a ponderosa-pine forest bordered the canyon. The forests would have provided lumber for building materials and food, such as deer and antelope. For an industrious and thrifty society these would have been sufficient resources to support the community. However, over the generations as the Anasazi harvested trees for building construction, they deforested the area. When the Anasazi depleted the trees in Chaco Canyon, they used the network of roads to bring trees from as far as seventy miles away. Eventually the Anasazi overharvested the distant trees as well. With little vegetation in this arid environment, wind and water eroded away the topsoil very quickly and increased water runoff. Without trees or wildlife and with diminished crop production, the community suffered. In the early twelfth century several years of severe drought conditions made food and water supplies even scarcer. The combination of a lack of vegetation and drought caused the water table to drop below the level of the wells, which would have rendered the irrigation system useless. Eventually the combination of events caused by natural and human factors forced the Anasazi to abandon their homes and move to environs that were more hospitable.[1]

Although we will never have a full explanation of why the Anasazi abandoned Chaco Canyon, it is likely that they were at least partially responsible for the demise of the community. The Anasazi's destruction of their habitat coupled with a lack of rain caused an environmental collapse that made the canyon uninhabitable. When the canyon resources could no longer meet the needs of a large community, the Anasazi were forced to vacate the once-hospitable canyon environment. The interaction between the natural environment and human activity stressed the environment beyond the point of recovery.

There may be some parallels between the Chaco Canyon and the Outer Banks of today. Although both are uniquely beautiful areas, they can be harsh and difficult environments for human habitation. Like the Anasazi, who suffered through drought years, Outer Bankers face natural disasters that can make coastal areas less hospitable. A hurricane can change a community's fortunes just as a lack of rain can. Most important, it appears that the Anasazi damaged their environment, just as residents and visitors are damaging the Outer Banks environment. The ecosystems of both Chaco Canyon and the Outer Banks can be sensitive to human manipulation. While it is unlikely that the Outer Banks will become uninhabitable anytime soon, the combination of human and natural forces could change the islands in ways that diminish the beguiling beauty of this coastal environment.

Living with Change in the Twenty-first Century

The shore-line environment is a microcosm of rhythmic change: tides rise and fall; beaches erode and accrete; sand dunes form and move; inlets open and close; and the barrier island migrates landward. The movement is part of an order that allows the barrier island to survive by yielding to the powerful forces of nature. This adaptability of a barrier island is a blessing and a curse. While adaptability allows survival, change can create uncertainty and losses for humans who want stability and protection for their valuable property. Therefore it is not surprising when humans attempt to create more-stable communities by altering the natural coastal environment.

We live on a planet of change. The summits of Switzerland's Jura Mountains are composed of limestone that was created in a shallow sea some 175 million years ago. One hundred and fifty million years ago dinosaurs grazed where today joggers circle New York's Central Park. Only 20,000 years ago ice sheets covered the land where today's cities sprout skyscrapers,

Nature sometimes sculpts abstract art, as in this photograph of Jockey's Ridge.
Courtesy of the National Park Service, Cape Hatteras National Seashore

and the sand that was to form the Outer Banks was scattered among the shoals and riverbeds. Barrier islands, however, are some of the most rapidly changing places on the planet, and the Outer Banks is more dynamic than most such regions. Islands, such as those in the Outer Banks, that move three-quarters of a mile in four centuries are mercurial in geologic time indeed.

The early Bankers tried to control and alter the environment out of necessity as they struggled to survive in an often-harsh environment. Native Americans, the first inhabitants, had little technology and were few in numbers, so that they would have had little impact on the island environment. The first European settlers made modest alterations to the barrier-island environment by introducing livestock, cutting trees, and dredging inlets. The small populations and simple tools limited the early islanders' impact.

In the twenty-first century we may be overdoing our struggle to control nature. The 1930s projects, such as dune stabilization and bridge construction, ushered in the rapid economic growth and changes that have transformed the Outer Banks. The planners of the 1930s dune-stabilization project realized that they needed to stabilize the Outer Banks in order to encourage economic development. Once bridges, roads, and ferries connected the islands to the mainland, economic development soon followed. The stabilization project, along with an infusion of government spending on infrastructure, has changed the Outer Banks into a healthy economy that thrives on tourism dollars. Policy makers in the 1930s could not have imagined how much the Outer Banks would change by the end of the century; but their hopes that the stabilization project would shore up and give new life to the Outer Banks were realized. With further encouragement from government policies, such as flood insurance, and rising incomes, populations have flocked to coastal areas.

Today, although there are limitations on our ability to control nature, we have the technology that allows us to alter the balance of a barrier island. In addition increasing numbers of people are living on and visiting the islands. Indeed this seems to be the season for being at the beach, and the crush of people has transformed much of the area into a mass of vacation homes, motels, restaurants, and shops. Bridges, which now tie the islands of the Outer Banks to the mainland like strings that hold kites from drifting away, usher over increasing numbers of people and their possessions each season. The threat from the increasing rate of sea-level rise intensifies the drama and creates a combination of factors that will lead to major environmental alterations.

It is not surprising that humans alter the island environment. Indeed we affect the environment in some way with each action. Even growing crops is, in a sense, a battle with nature. Human and natural forces will continue to alter the Outer Banks, but people have always created and adjusted to change and even recovered from major catastrophes. The differences today are that we are less willing to live with the changeable character of a barrier island and have the technology and resources to make significant alterations. However, as scientific knowledge has improved, people have better begun to understand and appreciate nature's rhythms and the complex interaction between human and nature. We now recognize that many human activities adversely affect the coastal environment that we value so much. The alterations of the island ecosystem by humans create consequences for human society as well as for the natural environment. Clearly the well-being of the coastal environment and that of coastal communities are inextricably linked.

However, even if we desired to return to the time when people adapted to the powerful forces that shape shorelines, we could not. We cannot walk in Eden once we have lost our innocence. The economic engine unleashed in the 1930s, which has been gathering steam since the 1960s, is not likely to be halted. However, we can control how development affects the environment, where development will occur, and what form development takes.

Thinking like a Barrier Island

Aldo Leopold, a twentieth-century conservationist, suggested that we should follow a land ethic that recognizes the importance of the entire biotic community—soils, water, plants, and animals. Leopold proposed that because the land is a community to which we belong, we have a moral obligation to treat the land with respect. To coexist successfully with a changing environment, Leopold suggested that we "think like a mountain."[2]

To explain what he meant by "thinking like a mountain," Leopold recounted an episode in which he and his companions, traveling in mountains in the Southwest, wildly shot into a pack of wolves. At the time, early in the twentieth century, wilderness was valued for the wildlife available for hunters. Because wolves killed deer, the standard Forest Service policy was to exterminate wolves whenever possible. Over time, however, Leopold came to realize that wolves, deer, trees—indeed all living organisms—were interconnected and that wolves were as necessary as deer were for a healthy mountain ecosystem. Without wolves to control deer herds, deer denuded vegetation, thus causing erosion of the mountain and the subsequent destruction of the community. Therefore the mountain understands that the howl of the wolf—fearful to many—is a call of survival and recognizes the conditions for survival.

Thinking more like a barrier island might help to create sustainable coastal communities. We might consider how a barrier island interprets the sounds of waves, which are portents of potential shore-line erosion. Just as wolves are necessary for a healthy mountain ecosystem, waves are necessary for a healthy barrier-island ecosystem. Waves, which cause coastal erosion, also create overwash, which allows islands to roll over themselves and to survive. Sand movement created by waves can lead to erosion but also to accretion as islands continually balance between the natural forces.

Perhaps we can limit the damage to coastal ecosystems by learning from the barrier island that adjusts to nature's rhythms. Trying to control inlets and using artificial means such as constructed dunes can be more costly than beneficial. Rather than armoring the shore with seawalls, a wise land-use policy should encourage the protection of the natural defenses of a barrier island. Sand dunes, natural buffers between shore and

Humankind shapes the Outer Banks with shore-line changes, such as housing development enabled by the 1930s sand-dune project.

sea, and vegetation, an important stabilizer of sand, should be protected. Removal of a shoreline's natural protection leads to erosion, just as removing vegetation on a mountain leads to erosion. Because barrier islands are valuable resources, limiting activities such as offshore oil drilling, which can detract from the natural beauty, may make good economic sense as well. Protecting coastal resources such as fisheries, waterways, and habitat areas may require changing incentive structures to control the "tragedy of the commons."

By understanding and acknowledging the dynamics of a barrier island, we can avoid coastal development that is shortsighted and destructive. Although the long-term trend of barrier-island migration and the potential danger from storms are well known, we continue to develop coastal areas. People should heed the information provided by geologists indicating which areas are subject to the most danger and avoid building in such locations. Although retreat may not be practical for areas that are heavily populated, areas that are most likely to be damaged but are not yet overly developed should be protected in their natural state.

We can encourage sustainable development with the proper use of incentives, even on a barrier island where change is so rapid. For example, when hurricanes continually batter an area, residents should be encouraged to relocate. In addition we should remove the subsidies and incentives that encourage activities that damage the environment. Providing subsidized flood insurance, beach nourishment, and infrastructure encourages individuals to locate in unstable areas such as an island oceanfront. In places that are suitable for development, property owners should understand and be willing to accept the risks and costs of their choices.

However, while we must be concerned about the changes that humans are creating on barrier islands, we must realize that the islands do not need to remain uninhabited. We should "live appropriately" but not expect islands to be pristine. Finding the proper mix of development and protection is the key.

The Outer Banks is an environment altered by sea, wind, and human choices, and it is irrevocably changed by the recent decades of development. If John White were exploring the coast today, would he still see the Outer Banks as "the goodliest and most pleasing territory of the world," as he did more than four centuries ago? The Outer Banks retains many of the qualities that must have appealed to White. The national park system protects 120 miles of shoreline, which is the longest stretch of undeveloped beach in the nation. Unfortunately development on the remaining portions often pollutes the water and land, destroys wildlife habitat, and crowds the land with congested communities. Unintentionally we are destroying the land that humans value so much.

Although the Outer Banks is unique, the problems are not. Many other coastal developments face similar changes and challenges brought on by the crush of humanity rushing to the beaches. Perhaps so many of us wish to be near the shore, particularly a barrier island, because it is a metaphor for new beginnings. We welcome the new beginnings that change brings: a shoreline washed smooth by the morning tide, the promise of a new year, leaving on a trip, the changing seasons. However, change can create uncertainty and anguish also: an eroding beach, a storm that washes away the foundations of homes built on sand, a death. Therefore we use all of our power and technology to try to control the alterations that we dislike. We can create temporary barriers against the sea by stabilizing beaches, inlets, and buildings. However, the stabilization process alters irrevocably the original coastal environment and changes the nature of the shore.

Outer Bankers have lived with change ever since they first chose to inhabit the strips of sand that shelter much of the North Carolina mainland. A rich history exists on these ribbons of sand where the wind and sea reshape the islands' contour daily and the shorelines reinvent themselves from moment to moment. On the land where the Lost Colony vanished,

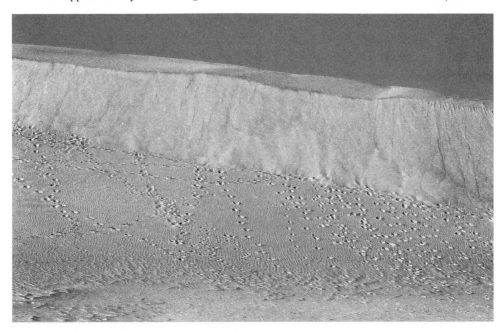

Footprints in the sand at Jockey's Ridge

Blackbeard terrorized citizens, and the Wright brothers introduced civilization to the wonders of flight, a culture interacts with its environment. Battered by some of the world's most devastating storms, living on sand that migrates toward the mainland, and faced with rising sea level that promises further erosion and flooding, Bankers persevere.

Life on the Outer Banks is about the interaction between human and nature and about adaptation to one's environment. As the Anasazi ruins at Chaco Canyon illustrate, there are limits to how much control humans can—or should—have over nature. Europeans began changing the Outer Banks as soon as they arrived, but the Outer Banks began changing those who came also. Change does not have to be destructive; both human and ecosystem can adapt and survive. Change can create opportunities and challenges to which we can respond with innovative policies that improve the quality of life. With some effort we can live in balance with the coastal environment and adapt to change. Change is, of course, the only certainty.

. . . .

. . . .

Notes

. . . .

Chapter One. **A Place Created by Change**

1. Barrier islands are elongated, dune-covered strips of sand that parallel the coastline.

2. Frankenberg, *The Nature of North Carolina's Southern Coast,* 3.

3. Dolan and Lins, *The Outer Banks of North Carolina.*

4. Frankenberg, *The Nature of the Outer Banks,* 29.

5. Diamond, *Guns, Germs, and Steel,* 25.

Chapter Two. **Change by Nature**

1. Bascom, *Waves and Beaches,* 187.

2. James Trefil, *A Scientist at the Seashore,* 131.

3. Pilkey et al., *The North Carolina Shore.*

4. Leatherman, *Barrier Islands Handbook,* 18.

5. Marsh, *Man and Nature,* 424.

6. Bascom, *Waves and Beaches,* 9.

7. Ibid., 244.

8. Inman and Dolan, "The Outer Banks of North Carolina."

9. Davis, *The Evolving Coast,* 182.

10. Frankenberg, *The Nature of the Outer Banks,* 69.

11. Mallinson et al., *Past, Present and Future Inlets of the Outer Banks,* 4.

12. Frankenberg, *The Nature of the Outer Banks,* 2.

13. Ibid., 49.

14. Actually "sea level" is an oxymoron. Because something is always disturbing the sea—waves, tides, winds—it is never level. To measure sea level means taking the average of all possible sea levels.

15. Davis, *The Evolving Coast,* 39.

16. Lennon et al., *Living with the South Carolina Coast,* 35.

17. Carlson, "The Bright Side of Hurricanes."

18. Zebrowski, *Perils of a Restless Planet,* 238.

19. Following a storm, walkers sometimes can see thick, black mats of vegetation and even tree stumps protruding from the beach. These are the remains of what had once been a marsh and maritime forest that had grown along the *back* side of the barrier beach.

Chapter Three. **Change by Humankind**

1. Schoenbaum, *Islands, Capes, and Sounds,* 19.
2. The first meeting between Native Americans and Europeans on the North Carolina coast took place during Verrazano's expedition in 1524. This friendly gathering probably occurred somewhere south of Cape Fear. Following an exchange of some gifts on the shore, Native Americans helped a sailor get back to his boat. As was the case in much of the Americas, however, Native Americans and settlers clashed often in this area, and ultimately the losers were Native Americans. Within two hundred years of Verrazano's first contact, Native American life and culture disappeared from the Outer Banks.
3. "More Evidence Found on Lost Colony."
4. More information on the wreck can be found at http://www.qaronline.org/ (accessed November 19, 2009).
5. Lencek and Bosker, *The Beach,* 157.
6. Stick, *The Outer Banks,* 96.
7. Ibid., 97.
8. Although the price increased from fifty cents per acre in the 1830s to sixty cents in 1866, when adjusted for inflation over that period, the *real* price of the land decreased.
9. Bishir, *The Unpainted Aristocracy,* 11.
10. Dunbar, *Historical Geography of the North Carolina Banks,* 18.
11. Spears, "The Sand Wave."
12. Many mainlanders continued to graze livestock on Shackleford well into the twentieth century until the federal government began management of the islands. Beginning in 1976, when Shackleford Banks became part of the Cape Lookout National Seashore, the Park Service removed the remaining sheep, goats, and cows that were grazing on the island. When the Park Service tried to remove a herd of horses, public concern stopped the removal. The horses remain on the island and continue to graze the dunes and salt marshes. Such grazing has devastated marshes on the backside of the island.
13. Stick, *The Outer Banks,* 242.
14. Ibid., 243.
15. Ibid., 246.
16. Ibid., 249.
17. During the Great Depression years such jobs were welcome. Indeed one might wonder whether the dune stabilization would have been completed if it were not for the Depression, which created an ample supply of workers willing to work for low wages.
18. Stratton, "Reclaiming the North Carolina Banks," 26–27.

19. Dolan and Lins, *The Outer Banks,* 21.

20. Ibid., 252.

21. Anderson and Hill, "Appropriable Rents from Yellowstone Park."

22. The bridge collapsed in 1990 when a barge struck it, and it was rebuilt within four months.

23. "Ten Best Surf Towns in America."

24. The developer proposed a twenty-two-bedroom house originally but changed the plan because ocean setback would have been 300 feet, not the 150 feet required for the smaller house. See Hewlett and Railey, "Built on Sand."

25. Ruffin, "The Wild Horses."

26. Palmquist et al., *Boating Uses.*

Chapter Four. **Understanding the "Sea of Troubles" Facing Coastal Communities**

1. Anderson and Hill, "From Free Grass to Fences."

2. King, "The Closing of the Southern Range."

3. Cattle grazing on Cedar Island caused an absence of dune development, while the ungrazed sections of the barrier island had dunes up to 3.5 meters in elevation (Barber and Pilkey, "Influence of Grazing on Barrier Island Vegetation").

4. Hardin, "The Tragedy of the Commons."

5. U.S. Commission on Ocean Policy, "Achieving Sustainable Fisheries," chapter 19 of *An Ocean Blueprint,* 3.

6. In 2004 both the U.S. Commission on Ocean Policy (a governmental panel) and the Pew Oceans Commission (a private panel) completed extensive studies on the state of ocean resources.

7. U.S. Commission on Ocean Policy, "Achieving Sustainable Fisheries," in *An Ocean Blueprint,* 3.

8. North Carolina Division of Marine Fisheries, "Statistics."

9. North Carolina Division of Marine Fisheries, "State Releases Report Card on Health of Fisheries."

10. Crossett et al., *Population Trends along the Coastal United States.*

11. Culliton, "Population Distribution Density and Growth."

12. Culliton et al., "50 Years of Population Change along the Nation's Coasts."

13. Federal Emergency Management Agency, "Policy and Claim Statistics for Flood Insurance."

14. Brower et al., *A Plan to Make Nags Head Less Vulnerable.*

15. H. John Heinz Center for Science, Economics and the Environment, *Evaluation of Erosion Hazards,* xxiv.

16. Pasterick, "The National Flood Insurance Program," 134.

17. David Conrad et al., "Higher Ground," in Palmquist et al., *Boating Uses.*

18. Esnard et al., "Coastal Hazards," 56.

19. H. John Heinz Center for Science, Economics and the Environment, *Evaluation of Erosion Hazards,* 26.

20. Scism, "Insurance Pool's Coverage to Coastal Carolina Ebbs."

21. Valverde et al., "Summary of Beach Nourishment Episodes."
22. National Oceanic and Atmospheric Administration, "Beach Nourishment."
23. U.S. Army Inspector General, "Report of Investigation."
24. Whitlock, "Flooded with Generosity."
25. Cordes and Yezer, "In Harm's Way."
26. Stick, *The Outer Banks.*
27. Fogarty, "To the Beach—or Bust?"
28. North Carolina Association of Realtors.
29. Thompson, "Oil Drilling Dispute Flares."
30. Although an oil spill from drilling has never occurred along the Outer Banks, during World War II, German U-boats sank many U.S. ships, which spilled some 150 million gallons of oil on the Outer Banks shores.
31. Palmquist et al., *Boating Uses,* 3.
32. Ibid.
33. Mineral Management Service, "Manteo Exploration Unit."
34. Shiffer, "Last Oil Leases off N.C. Relinquished."
35. Laskin, "Land of the Free, Home of Bad Weather."
36. Stick, *The Outer Banks,* 192.
37. Blake et al., *The Deadliest, Costliest, and Most Intense United States Tropical Cyclones from 1851 to 2006.*
38. Horn, *The Katrina Disaster.*
39. Esnard et al., "Coastal Hazards."
40. Goldenberg et al., "The Recent Increase in Atlantic Hurricane Activity."
41. Pielke et al., "Normalized Hurricane Damages."
42. Campo-Flores, "The Swirling Winds of Politics."
43. Kunreuther and Michel-Kerjan, *Managing Large Scale Risks,* 78.
44. Kozak, "Insurance Rates on the Coast."
45. Grace and Klein, "Facing Mother Nature."
46. Pielke and Pielke, *Hurricanes,* 120.
47. Miletti, *Disaster by Design.*
48. Baish et al., "Coastal Erosion."
49. Stanley Riggs et al., *North Carolina's Coasts in Crisis.*
50. Parry et al., "Technical Summary."
51. Kerr, "Pushing the Scary Side of Global Warming."
52. A coastal geomorphology rule of thumb, the "Bruun Rule," predicts that a 1-centimeter rise in sea level will cause a 50- to 80-centimeter increase in horizontal beach erosion; if correct, this would suggest that an increase of 1 meter (or about 3 feet) in sea-level rise would lead to 150 to 240 feet of erosion. However, there is debate concerning the relevancy of the model. See Bruun, "The Bruun Rule of Erosion."
53. Mazria and Kershner, *Nation under Siege.*
54. Stanley Riggs and Ames, "Drowning the North Carolina Coast."
55. Whitehead et al., "Measuring the Impacts of Sea Level Rise."
56. Trenberth, "Warmer Oceans, Stronger Hurricanes."

57. Knutson et al., "Simulated Reduction in Atlantic Hurricane Frequency."

58. Bin et al., *Measuring the Impacts of Climate Change.*

Chapter Five. Attempts at Controlling Change by Nature

1. Alexander and Lazell, *Ribbons of Sand,* 54–55.

2. Schoenbaum, *Islands, Capes, and Sounds,* 201.

3. The dredge *Northerly Island* experienced the difficult channel currents on October 26, 1990, when it drifted into the Herbert C. Bonner Bridge, which connects Hatteras and Bodie islands. The dredge was part of an annual $4.4 million ACE program to dredge seven hundred thousand cubic yards of sand from the inlet. Although nobody was injured, the bridge collapsed into the inlet. It took almost four months to reconstruct the bridge, which provides the only road between the islands.

4. Pilkey and Dixon, *The Corps and the Shore,* 197.

5. Ibid., 217–19.

6. Ibid., 192.

7. Ibid., 215.

8. Ibid., 199–204.

9. Allegood, "Jetty Debate Swelling Anew."

10. Grunwald, "The Corps Cored."

11. Council on Environmental Quality, "Federal Agencies Reach Consensus."

12. Stanley Riggs et al., *North Carolina's Coasts in Crisis.*

13. "Back to Bonner."

14. Stratton and Hollowell, *Methods of Sand Fixation,* 90.

15. Ibid., 96–102.

16. Wirth, "A Letter to the People of the Outer Banks."

17. Birkemeier et al., "The Evolution of a Barrier Island."

18. Robert Dolan et al., "Man's Impact on the Barrier Islands."

19. Dolan and Lins, *The Outer Banks.*

20. Dolan et al., "Man's Impact on the Barrier Islands," 159.

21. Ibid., 152.

22. Stick, *The Outer Banks.*

23. Senter, "Live Dunes and Ghost Forests."

24. Stratton and Hollowell, *Methods of Sand Fixation,* 90.

25. Dolan et al., "Man's Impact on the Barrier Islands."

26. Behn and Clark, "Termination of Beach Erosion Control," 117.

27. National Park Service, "Environmental Assessment."

28. Behn and Clark, "Termination of Beach Erosion Control."

29. Stratton, "Reclaiming the North Carolina Banks," 25.

30. Stanley Riggs et al., *North Carolina's Coasts in Crisis.*

31. Pilkey et al., *The North Carolina Shore,* 139.

32. Ibid., 6.

33. Pilkey and Dixon, *The Corps and the Shore,* 245.

34. Horan, "Inch by Inch."

35. Stratton and Hollowell, *Methods of Sand Fixation,* 90.

Chapter Six. **Living with Change in Coastal Communities**

1. Colgan, "The Changing Ocean and Coastal Economy."
2. Dalesio, "North Carolina Sets Home Size Rules for Coast."
3. Alexander and Lazell, *Ribbons of Sand,* 96–108.
4. North Carolina General Statute 113A-100 et seq.
5. Heath and Owens, "Coastal Management Law in North Carolina," 1426.
6. Godschalk, "Implementing Coastal Zone Management."
7. Rawlins, "Beach Protection in North Carolina a Façade."
8. Norton, "More and Better Local Planning."
9. Platt et al., "Rebuilding the North Carolina Coast."
10. North Carolina Coastal Federation, "North Topsail Beach."
11. Pompe and Rinehart, "The Lucas Case and the Conflict over Property Rights."
12. In another takings issue, in Long Branch, New Jersey, property owners challenged the right of government to use eminent domain to take coastal property for economic development. This follows the June 2005 decision by the U.S. Supreme Court declaring that the city of New London, Connecticut, had the right to take private property and give it to private developers if the local economy benefited.
13. Pompe and Lipford, "Putting Private Lands into Public Hands."
14. Porter and Salvesen, *Collaborative Planning for Wetlands and Wildlife,* 101.
15. Pasterick, "The National Flood Insurance Program," 152.
16. Kunreuther, "Has the Time Come?"
17. H. John Heinz Center for Science, Economics and the Environment, *Evaluation of Erosion Hazards,* 22.
18. Thieler and Hammar-Klose, *National Assessment of Coastal Vulnerability.*
19. Blake et al., *The Deadliest, Costliest, and Most Intense United States Tropical Cyclones.*
20. Fronstin and Holtman, "The Determinants of Residential Property Damage"; Rogers and Tezak, "Hurricane Isabel Damage," 38.
21. McLeister, "Lessons from Katrina."
22. Rogers and Tezak, "Hurricane Isabel Damage," 43.
23. Costanza and Farber, *The Economic Value of Wetlands,* 112.
24. Pilkey et al., *The North Carolina Shore.*
25. Rogers, "Relocating Erosion Threatened Buildings."
26. Titus, "Rising Seas, Coastal Erosion and the Takings Clause."
27. Stanley Riggs et al., *North Carolina's Coasts in Crisis.*
28. Trebanis et al., "Comparison of Beach Nourishment."
29. Parsons and Powell ("Measuring the Cost of Beach Retreat") examine the issue of whether retreat or nourishment is more economical. They estimate the cost over the next fifty years of allowing Delaware's ocean beaches to retreat inland. If erosion rates remain at historic levels, they estimate that the cost of lost land and capital (such as housing) over the next fifty years in present value terms is about $291 million. They conclude that nourishing beaches, at least over this time period, is less expensive than retreat.

30. Determining the value of nonmarket goods such as the recreational benefit from wider beaches is sometimes difficult. One approach is the hedonic pricing method that uses statistical methods to determine the value of a particular characteristic. For example, if two houses are the same but one house is located in an area with a wider beach, the price of the house with the wider beach will be higher. Using statistical methods, one could adjust for other differences in the two houses and estimate the value of the wider beach. An example of this method can be found in Pompe and Rinehart, "The Value of Beach Nourishment to Property Owners."

31. Ibid.

32. Ledoux, "Beach Project Outlined."

33. Pompe, "The Nature of Sand."

34. Bush et al., *Living by the Rules of the Sea,* 74–75.

35. Young and Coburn, "Sandbag Seawalls Do More Harm than Good."

36. Platt et al., "Rebuilding the North Carolina Coast," 252.

37. Barnet and Hill, "Design for Rising Sea Levels."

38. American Society of Civil Engineers, "The New Orleans Hurricane Protection System."

39. North Carolina. Session Law 2005-442.

40. Collins, "Study Sees Boom in Climate Change."

41. Mills and Lecomte, *From Risk to Opportunity.*

42. David Riggs, "Market Incentives for Water Quality."

43. North Carolina Clean Water Management Trust Fund, "Fact Sheet."

44. North Carolina Division of Marine Fisheries, 2005 *Coastal Habitat Protection Plan.*

45. Pompe and Rinehart, *Environmental Conflict.*

46. Pompe and Rinehart, "Entrepreneurship and Coastal Resource Management."

47. U.S. Commission on Ocean Policy, *An Ocean Blueprint,* 288.

48. Dean, "Bush Forms Panel to Coordinate Ocean Policy."

49. Stick, ed., *The Outer Banks Reader,* 55.

Chapter Seven. Time and Chance

1. Cloud, *Portsmouth,* 3.

2. Stick, *The Outer Banks,* 45.

3. Cloud, *Portsmouth,* 84–86.

4. Stick, ed., *The Outer Banks Reader.*

5. Stick, *The Outer Banks,* 301.

6. Salter, *Portsmouth Island.*

Chapter Eight. An Apprenticeship with Change

1. Diamond, "The Golden Age That Never Was."

2. Leopold, *Sand County Almanac.*

Bibliography

. . . .

Alexander, John, and James Lazell. *Ribbons of Sand*. Chapel Hill, N.C.: Algonquin Books of Chapel Hill, 1992.

Allegood, Jerry. "Jetty Debate Swelling Anew." *Raleigh News and Observer*, June 19, 2000, A1.

American Society of Civil Engineers. "The New Orleans Hurricane Protection System: What Went Wrong and Why." Report by the American Society of Civil Engineers Hurricane Katrina External Review Panel, 2007.

Anderson, Terry L., and Peter J. Hill. "Appropriable Rents from Yellowstone Park: A Case of Incomplete Contracting." *Economic Inquiry* 34 (1996): 506–18.

———. "From Free Grass to Fences: Transforming the Commons of the American West." In *Managing the Commons*, edited by John A. Baden and Douglas S. Noonan. Bloomington: Indiana University Press, 1998.

Bachman, Karen. *Insiders' Guide to North Carolina's Outer Banks*. Guilford, Conn.: Globe Pequot, 2005.

"Back to Bonner." *Raleigh News and Observer*, May 9, 2009. Available at www.news observer.com/opinion/editorials/story/76594.html (accessed December 13, 2009).

Baish, S., S. Dunn, and R. Friedman. "Coastal Erosion: Evaluating the Risk." *Environment* 22, no. 7 (2000): 36–45.

Ballance, Alton. *Ocracokers*. Chapel Hill: University of North Carolina Press, 1989.

Barber, D. C., and O. H. Pilkey Jr. "Influence of Grazing on Barrier Island Vegetation and Geomorphology, Coastal North Carolina." Geological Society of America Annual Meeting, November 1–10, 2001, Boston, paper no. 68.

Barnes, Jay. *North Carolina Hurricane History*. Chapel Hill: University of North Carolina Press, 1998.

Barnet, J., and K. Hill. "Design for Rising Sea Levels." *Harvard Design Magazine* 27 (Fall 2007 / Winter 2008): 1–7.

Bascom, Willard. *Waves and Beaches: The Dynamics of the Ocean Surface*. Garden City, N.Y.: Anchor Books, 1964.

Bedwell, Dorothy Byrum. *Portsmouth: Island with a Soul*. New Bern, N.C.: IES Publications, 1984.

Behn, Robert D., and Martha A. Clark. "The Termination of Beach Erosion Control at Cape Hatteras." *Public Policy* 27, no. 1 (1979): 99–127.

Bin, Okmyung, Chris Dumas, Ben Poulter, and John Whitehead. *Measuring the Impacts of Climate Change on North Carolina Coastal Resources*. Final report, March 15, 2007. Washington, D.C.: National Commission on Energy Policy, 2007.

Birkemeier, William, Robert Dolan, and Nina Fisher. "The Evolution of a Barrier Island: 1930–1980." *Shore and Beach* 52 (April 1984): 2–12.

Bishir, Catherine. *The Unpainted Aristocracy: The Beach Cottages of Old Nags Head*. Raleigh: Division of Archives and History, North Carolina Department of Cultural Resources, 1980.

Blake, E. S., E. N. Rappaport, and C. W. Landsea. *The Deadliest, Costliest, and Most Intense United States Tropical Cyclones from 1851 to 2006 (and Other Frequently Requested Hurricane Facts)*. NOAA Technical Memorandum NWS TPC-5. Miami: National Weather Service, April 2007.

Brower, David, A. K. Schwab, and Bruce Bortz. *A Plan to Make Nags Head Less Vulnerable to the Impacts of Natural Hazards*. Prepared for the Nags Head Board of Commissioners, 1998.

Bruun, P. "The Bruun Rule of Erosion by Sea-Level Rise: A Discussion on Large-Scale Two- and Three-Dimensional Usages." *Journal of Coastal Research* 4, no. 4 (1988): 627–48.

Bunyea, Charley. "With Voting Ongoing, so Is the Debate on Beach Nourishment." *Outer Banks Sentinel*, February 2006. Available at http://obsentinel.womack newspapers.com/articles/2006/02/01/top_stories/tops334101.prt (accessed November 27, 2009).

Bush, David, Orrin Pilkey, and William Neal. *Living by the Rules of the Sea*. Durham, N.C.: Duke University Press, 1996.

Campo-Flores, Arian. "The Swirling Winds of Politics." *Newsweek*, September 20, 2004, 8.

Carlson, Peter. "The Bright Side of Hurricanes." *Washington Post*, September 19, 2003.

Cicin-Sain, B., and R. Knecht. *Integrated Coastal and Ocean Management: Concepts and Practices*. Washington, D.C.: Island Press, 1998.

Cloud, Ellen Fulcher. *Portsmouth: The Way It Was*. Havelock, N.C.: Print Shop, 1996.

Colgan, Charles S. "The Changing Ocean and Coastal Economy of the United States." Prepared for the National Governors Association Center for Best Practices, October 2003.

Collins, Kristin. "Study Sees Boom in Climate Change." *Raleigh News and Observer*, October 24, 2007, B5.

Cordes, Joseph J., and Anthony M. J. Yezer. "In Harm's Way: Does Federal Spending on Beach Enhancement and Protection Induce Excessive Development in Coastal Areas?" *Land Economics* 74 (February 1998): 128–45.

Costanza, R., R. d'Arge, R. de Groot, S. Farber, M. Grasso, B. Hannon, K. Limburg, et al. "The Value of the World's Ecosystem Services and Natural Capital." *Ecological Economics* 25, no. 1 (1998): 3–15.

Council on Environmental Quality. "Federal Agencies Reach Consensus Ending Development of the Oregon Inlet Jetty Proposal." May 1, 2003. Available at http://georgewbush-whitehouse.archives.gov/news/releases/2003/05/20030501-17 .html (accessed January 20, 2010).

Crossett, K. M., T. J. Culliton, P. C. Wiley, and T. R. Goodspeed. *Population Trends along the Coastal United States: 1980–2008.* Silver Spring, Md.: National Oceanic and Atmospheric Administration, NOAA's National Ocean Service, Special Projects, 2004.

Culliton, Thomas. "Population: Distribution, Density and Growth." NOAA's State of the Coast Report. Silver Spring, Md.: National Oceanic and Atmospheric Administration, 1998. Available at http://oceanservice.noaa.gov/websites/retired sites/sotc_pdf/POP.PDF (accessed November 27, 2009).

Culliton, Thomas, Maureen Warren, Timothy Goodspeed, Davida Remer, Carol Blackwell, and John McDonough. "50 Years of Population Change along the Nation's Coasts, 1960–2010." U.S. Department of Commerce, National Oceanic and Atmospheric Administration, April 1990.

Cummings, William. *The Southeast in Early Maps.* Chapel Hill: University of North Carolina Press, 1998.

Dalesio, Emery P. "North Carolina Sets Home Size Rules for Coast." *State* (Columbia, S.C.), September 11, 2003, B6.

Davis, Richard. *The Evolving Coast.* New York: Scientific American Library, 1994.

Dean, Cornelia. *Against the Tide: The Battle for America's Beaches.* New York: Columbia University Press, 1999.

———. "Bush Forms Panel to Coordinate Ocean Policy." *New York Times,* December 18, 2004. Available at www.pewoceanscience.org/press/media-coverage-article (accessed November 27, 2009).

Deblieu, Jan. *Hatteras Journal.* Winston-Salem, N.C.: John F. Blair, 1998.

Diamond, Jared. "The Golden Age That Never Was." *Discover* 9 (December 1988): 70–79.

———. *Guns, Germs, and Steel.* New York: W. W. Norton, 1998.

Dolan, Robert. "Experiences with Atlantic Coast Storms." *Shore and Beach* 5 (July 1996): 3–7.

Dolan, Robert, and Harry Lins. *The Outer Banks of North Carolina.* U.S. Geological Survey Professional Paper 1177-B. Washington, D.C.: U.S. Government Printing Office, 1986.

Dolan, Robert, William Odum, and Paul Godfrey. "Man's Impact on the Barrier Island of North Carolina." *American Scientist,* March–April 1973, 161–62.

Dunbar, Gary. *Historical Geography of the North Carolina Banks.* Baton Rouge: Louisiana State University Press, 1958.

Esnard, Ann-Margaret, David Bower, and Bruce Bortz. "Coastal Hazards and the Built Environment on Barrier Islands: A Retrospective View of Nags Head in the Late 1990s." *Coastal Management* 29 (2001): 53–72.

Federal Emergency Management Agency. "Policy and Claim Statistics for Flood Insurance." Available at http://www.fema.gov/business/nfip/statistics/pcstat.shtm (accessed November 27, 2009).

Fogarty, Thomas A. "To the Beach—or Bust?" *USA Today*, August 13, 2003. Available at www.usatoday.com/money/perfi/housing/2003-08-13-summerhome_x.htm (accessed November 28, 2009).

Fox, William T. *At the Sea's Edge*. Englewood Cliffs, N.J.: Prentice-Hall, 1983.

Frankenberg, Dirk. *The Nature of North Carolina's Southern Coast: Barrier Islands, Coastal Waters, and Wetlands*. Chapel Hill: University of North Carolina Press, 1997.

———. *The Nature of the Outer Banks*. Chapel Hill: University of North Carolina Press, 1995.

Fronstin, P., and A. G. Holtman. "The Determinants of Residential Property Damage Caused by Hurricane Andrew." *Southern Economic Journal* 61 (1994): 387–97.

Godschalk, David. "Implementing Coastal Zone Management: 1972–1990." *Coastal Management* 20, no. 2 (1992): 93–166.

Godschalk, David, Timothy Beatley, Phillip Berkes, David Brower, and Edward Kaisen. *Natural Hazard Mitigation*. Washington, D.C.: Island Press, 1999.

Godschalk, David, David Brown, and Timothy Beatley. *Catastrophic Coastal Storms*. Durham, N.C.: Duke University Press, 1989.

———. *Coastal Hazards Mitigation: Public Notification, Expenditure Limitations, and Hazard Areas Acquisition*. Chapel Hill: University of North Carolina Center for Urban and Regional Studies, 1998.

Goldenberg, Stanley B., Christopher W. Landsea, Alberto M. Mestas-Nunoz, and William M. Gray. "The Recent Increase in Atlantic Hurricane Activity: Causes and Implications." *Science* 293 (July 20, 2001): 474–79.

Grace, M. F., and R. W. Klein. "Facing Mother Nature." *Regulation* 30 (Fall 2007): 28–34.

Grunwald, Michael. "The Corps Cored." May 5, 2003. Available at Slate.msn.com/id/2082577 (accessed November 29, 2009).

H. John Heinz Center for Science, Economics and the Environment. *Evaluation of Erosion Hazards*. Prepared for the Federal Emergency Management Agency Contract EMW-97–CO-0375. April 2000.

———. *The Hidden Costs of Coastal Hazards: Implications for Risk Assessment and Mitigation*. Washington, D.C.: Island Press, 2000.

Hardin, Garret. "The Tragedy of Commons." *Science* 162 (December 13, 1968): 1243–48.

Hariot, Thomas. *A Briefe and True Report of New Found Land of Virginia*. London, 1588. Reprint, New York: Arno Press, 1972.

Heath, Milton, Jr., and David W. Owens. "Coastal Management Law in North Carolina: 1974–1994." *North Carolina Law Review* 72 (1993–94): 1413–51.

Hewlett, Michael, and John Railey. "Built on Sand: Damage Renews Development Debate." *Winston Salem Journal*, September 22, 2003, A1.

Horan, Jack. "Inch by Inch." *Charlotte Observer*, June 6, 1999, A7.

Horn, Geoffrey. *The Katrina Disaster*. Available at www.history.com/encyclopedia.do?articleId=227896 (accessed January 20, 2010).

Howe, Jim, Ed McMahon, and Luther Propst. *Balancing Nature and Communities in Gateway Communities.* Washington, D.C.: Island Press, 1997.

Hulton, Paul. *America 1585: The Complete Drawings of John White.* Chapel Hill: University of North Carolina Press, 1984.

Inman, D., and R. Dolan. "The Outer Banks of North Carolina: Budget of Sediment and Inlet Dynamics along a Migratory Barrier Island System." *Journal of Coastal Research* 5, no. 2 (1989): 193–237.

Kerr, R. A. "Pushing the Scary Side of Global Warming." *Science* 316, no. 5830 (2007): 1412–15.

King, J. Crawford. "The Closing of the Southern Range: An Exploratory Study." *Journal of Southern History* 48, no. 1 (1982): 53–70.

Knutson, Thomas R., Joseph J. Sirutis, Stephen T. Garner, Gabriel A. Vecchi, and Isaac M. Held. "Simulated Reduction in Atlantic Hurricane Frequency under Twenty-First-Century Warming Conditions." *Nature Geoscience,* May 18, 2008.

Kozak, Catherine. "Insurance Rates on the Coast to Jump if Plan Approved." December 2008. Hamptonroads.com.

Kriesel, Warren, and Craig Landry. "Participation in the National Flood Insurance Program: An Empirical Analysis for Coastal Properties." *Journal of Risk and Insurance* 71 (September 2004): 405–20.

Kunreuther, Howard C. "Has the Time Come?" In *On Risk and Disaster: Lessons from Hurricane Katrina,* edited by R. J. Daniels, D. F. Kettl, and H. Kunreuther. Philadelphia: University of Pennsylvania Press, 2006.

Kunreuther, Howard C., and E. O. Michel-Kerjan, directors. *Managing Large Scale Risks in a New Era of Catastrophes: Insuring, Mitigating, and Financing Recovery from Natural Disasters in the United States.* Philadelphia: University of Pennsylvania, Wharton Risk Management and Decisions Processes Center, March 2008.

Laskin, David. *Braving the Elements: The Stormy History of American Weather.* New York: Doubleday, 1997.

———. "Land of the Free, Home of Bad Weather," *Wall Street Journal,* September 16, 1999. Available at www.junkscience.com/sep99/weather.html (accessed December 6, 2009).

Leatherman, Stephen P. *Barrier Islands Handbook.* Coastal Publication Series. Baltimore: University of Maryland Press, 1988.

Ledoux, Julia. "Beach Project Outlined." *Outer Banks Sentinel* (Nags Head, N.C.), January 9, 2005. Available at sc.coastalscience.com/projects/press/050109 _news_obsent_nags.pdf (accessed December 1, 2009).

Lencek, Lena, and Gideon Bosker. *The Beach: The History of Paradise on Earth.* New York: Viking Penguin, 1998.

Lennon, Gered, William Neal, David Bush, Orrin Pilkey, Matthew Stutz, and Jane Bullock. *Living with the South Carolina Coast.* Durham, N.C.: Duke University Press, 1996.

Leopold, Aldo. *Sand County Almanac.* New York: Ballantine Books, 1970.

Ludlum, David. *Early American Hurricanes 1492–1870.* Boston: American Meteorological Society, 1963.

MacLeish, William. *Gulf Stream: Encounters with the Blue God.* Boston: Houghton Mifflin, 1989.

Mallinson, David J., Stephen J. Culver, Stanley R. Riggs, J. P. Walsh, Dorothea Ames, and Curtis W. Smith. *Past, Present and Future Inlets of the Outer Banks Barrier Islands, North Carolina.* North Carolina Coastal Geology Cooperative Research Program White Paper, 2008.

Marsh, George P. *Man and Nature.* 1864. New edition, edited by David Lowenthal. Cambridge, Mass.: Belknap Press of Harvard University Press, 1967.

Mazria, Edward, and Kristina Kershner. *Nation under Siege: Sea Level Rise at Our Doorstep.* The 2030 Research Center, 2007. Available at http://architecture2030.org/pdfs/nation_under_siege_lr.pdf (accessed January 20, 2010).

McLeister, D. "Lessons from Katrina: Better Building, Codes, Materials." July 7, 2007. Available at www.hgtvpro.com/hpro/nws_dstr_huric_torndo/article/ 0,2624,HPRO_265224503255,00.html (accessed November 29, 2009).

Miletti, Dennis. *Disaster by Design: A Reassessment of Natural Hazards in the United States.* Washington, D.C.: John Henry Press, 1999.

Mills, E., and E. Lecomte. *From Risk to Opportunity: How Insurers Can Proactively and Profitably Manage Climate Change.* Boston, Mass.: Ceres, 2006.

Mineral Management Service. "Manteo Exploration Unit OCS Leases Offshore North Carolina." August 29, 2001. Available at www.gomr.mms.gov/homepg/offshore/atlocs/manteo.html (accessed November 30, 2009).

"More Evidence Found on Lost Colony." *State* (Columbia, S.C.), October 18, 1998, A10.

Myers, Ransom A., and Boris Worm. "Rapid Worldwide Depletion of Predatory Fish Communities." *Nature* 423 (May 15, 2003): 280–83.

National Oceanic and Atmospheric Administration (NOAA). "Beach Nourishment." Available at http://www.csc.noaa.gov/beachnourismnent/ (accessed January 20, 2010).

National Park Service. "Environmental Assessment, Cape Hatteras Shoreline Erosion Policy Statement." Prepared by Denver Service Center. Atlanta, 1974, 73–122.

National Weather Service. "Summary of the 2004 Season." U.S. Department of Commerce. Available at www.hurricaneville.com/2004.html (accessed November 30, 2009).

Nordstrom, Karl F. *Beaches and Dunes of Developed Coasts.* Cambridge: Cambridge University Press, 2000.

North Carolina. Session Law 2005-442. Available at http://www.ncga.state.nc.us/Sessions/2005/Bills/Senate/HTML/S1134v7.html (accessed December 3, 2009).

North Carolina Association of Realtors. "Year-End Statistics." Available at http://www.ncrealtors.org/market_statistics.cfm (accessed December 3, 2009).

North Carolina Clean Water Management Trust Fund. "Fact Sheet." 2008. Available at http://www.cwmtf.net/ (accessed December 3, 2009).

North Carolina Coastal Federation. "North Topsail Beach: Public Policy Gone Awry." 2003. Available at http://www.nccoast.org/publication/socreports/soc_03/pg12–13.pdf (accessed December 3, 2009).

North Carolina Division of Marine Fisheries. *North Carolina Oyster Fishery Management Plan.* Morehead City, N.C., August 2001.

———. "State Releases Report Card on Health of Fisheries." June 5, 2005. Available at www.ncdmf.net/stocks/index.html (accessed December 3, 2009).

———. "Statistics." Available at http://www.ncfisheries.net/statistics/index.htm (accessed December 3, 2009).

———. 2005 *Coastal Habitat Protection Plan.* Morehead City, N.C., 2005.

Norton, Richard K. "More and Better Local Planning: State-Mandated Local Planning in Coastal North Carolina." *Journal of the American Planning Association* 71 (January 2005): 55–71.

Olson, Sarah. *Historic Resource Study: Portsmouth Village, Cape Lookout National Seashore.* Washington, D.C.: U.S. Department of the Interior, 1982.

Palmquist, Raymond B., Peter W. Schuman, and Jeffrey A. Michael. *Boating Uses, Economic Significance, and Information Inventory for North Carolina's Offshore Area, "The Point."* Minerals Management Service Contract 1435-01-98-CA-30949. August 2002.

Parry, M. L., O. F. Canziani, J. P. Palutikof, et al. "Technical Summary." In *Climate Change 2007: Impacts, Adaptation and Vulnerability; Contribution of Working Group II to the Fourth Assessment Report of the Intergovernmental Panel on Climate Change,* edited by M. L. Parry, O. F. Canziani, J. P. Palutikof, P. J. van der Linden, and C. E. Hanson, 23–78. Cambridge: Cambridge University Press, 2007.

Parsons, George, and Michael Powell. "Measuring the Cost of Beach Retreat." *Coastal Management* 29 (2001): 91–103.

Pasterick, Edward. "The National Flood Insurance Program." In *Paying the Price: The Status and Role of Insurance against Natural Disasters in the United States,* edited by Howard Kunreuther and Richard J. Roth Sr. Washington, D.C.: Joseph Henry Press, 1998.

Pew Oceans Commission. *America's Living Oceans: Charting a Course for Sea Change.* Arlington, Va., May 2003.

Pielke, Roger, Jr., and Roger Pielke Sr. *Hurricanes: Their Nature and Impact on Society.* New York: Wiley, 1997.

Pielke, Roger A., Jr., Joel Gratz, Christopher W. Landsea, Douglas Collins, Mark A. Saunders, and Rade Musulin. "Normalized Hurricane Damages in the United States: 1900–2005." *Natural Hazards Review* 9 (February 2008): 29–42.

Pilkey, Orrin H., and Katherine L. Dixon. *The Corps and the Shore.* Washington, D.C.: Island Press, 1996.

Pilkey, Orrin H., and M. E. Fraser. *A Celebration of the World's Barrier Islands.* New York: Columbia University Press, 2003.

Pilkey, Orrin H., William J. Neal, Stanley R. Riggs, Craig A. Webb, and Brian A. Cowan. *The North Carolina Shore and Its Barrier Islands: Restless Ribbons of Sand.* Durham, N.C.: Duke University Press, 1998.

Platt, R. *Disasters and Democracies.* Washington, D.C.: Island Press, 1999.

———. "Evolution of Coastal Hazards Policies in the United States." *Coastal Management* 22 (1995): 265–84.

Platt, R., David Salvesen, and George Baldwin II. "Rebuilding the North Carolina Coast after Hurricane Fran: Did Public Regulations Matter?" *Coastal Management* 30 (July–September 2002): 249–69.

Pompe, Jeffrey. "The Nature of Sand: South Carolina's Shifting Shoreline." *South Carolina Policy Forum* 6 (Summer 1995): 4–12.

Pompe, Jeffrey, and Jody Lipford. "Putting Private Lands into Public Hands: Explaining Voter Choices to Purchase Public Lands." *Journal of Private Enterprise* 20 (Spring 2005): 1–26.

Pompe, Jeffrey, and James R. Rinehart. "Entrepreneurship and Coastal Resource Management." In *Re-Thinking Green,* edited by Carl Close and Robert Higgs. Oakland, Calif.: Independent Institute, 2005.

———. *Environmental Conflict: In Search of Common Ground.* Albany: State University of New York Press, 2002.

———. "The Lucas Case and the Conflict over Property Rights." In *Land Rights: The 1990s' Property Rights Rebellion,* edited by Bruce Yandle. Lanham, Md.: Rowman & Littlefield, 1995.

———. "The Value of Beach Nourishment to Property Owners: Storm Damage Reduction Benefits." *Review of Regional Studies* 25 (Winter 1995): 271–87.

Porter, Douglas, and David Salvesen, eds. *Collaborative Planning for Wetlands and Wildlife: Issues and Examples.* Washington, D.C.: Island Press, 1995.

Power, Thomas. *Lost Landscapes and Failed Economics.* Washington, D.C.: Island Press, 1996.

Rawlins, Wade. "Beach Protection in North Carolina a Façade." *Raleigh News and Observer,* July 5, 2003, A1.

Riggs, David. "Market Incentives for Water Quality." In *The Market Meets the Environment: Economic Analysis of Environmental Policy,* edited by Bruce Yandle. Lanham, Md.: Rowman & Littlefield, 1999.

Riggs, Stanley R., and D. V. Ames. "Drowning the North Carolina Coast: Sea-Level Rise and Estuarine Dynamic." North Carolina Sea Grant College Program, Raleigh, N.C., 2003, pub. no. UNC-SG-03–04.

Riggs, Stanley R., Stephen J. Culver, Dorothea V. Ames, David J. Mallinson, D. Reide Corbett, and J. P. Walsh. *North Carolina's Coasts in Crisis: A Vision for the Future.* North Carolina Coastal Geology Cooperative Research Program, 2008. Available at http://www.ecu.edu/geology/NCCoastsinCrisis.pdf (accessed December 4, 2009).

Rogers, Spencer M. "Relocating Erosion Threatened Buildings: A Study of North Carolina Housemoving." In *Coastal Zone 93,* edited by O. T. Magoon, W. S. Wilson, H. Converse, and L. T. Tobin, 1392–1405. New York: American Society of Civil Engineers, 1993.

Rogers, Spencer M., and E. Scott Tezak. "Hurricane Isabel Damage to Coastal North Carolina Buildings." *Shore and Beach* 72 (Spring 2004): 38–44.

Ruffin, Edmund. "The Wild Horses, Their Qualities and Habits." In *Agricultural, Geological, and Descriptive Sketches of Lower North Carolina and the Similar Adjacent Lands,* 130–33. Raleigh: Privately printed, 1861.

Safina, Carl. *Song for the Blue Ocean: Encounters along the World's Coasts and beneath the Seas.* New York: Henry Holt, 1998.

Salter, Ben. *Portsmouth Island: Short Stories and History.* Atlantic, N.C., 1972.

Schoenbaum, Thomas. *Islands, Capes, and Sounds.* Winston-Salem, N.C.: John F. Blair, 1982.

Scism, Leslie. "Insurance Pool's Coverage to Coastal Carolina Ebbs." *Wall Street Journal,* September 14, 2009. Available at http://online.wsj.com/article/S2528860 3617007331.html (accessed December 28, 2009)

Senter, Jim. "Live Dunes and Ghost Forests: Stability and Change in the History of North Carolina's Maritime Forests." *North Carolina Historical Review* 80 (July 2003): 334–71.

Shiffer, James Eli. "Last Oil Leases off N.C. Relinquished." *Raleigh News and Observer,* November 21, 2000, A3.

"Should Building Codes Be Strengthened in Zones Prone to Hurricanes?" *Wall Street Journal,* September 6, 1999, 1.

Spears, John R. "The Sand Wave." *Scribner's Wave* 8 (October 1890): 193–237.

Stick, David. *The Outer Banks of North Carolina.* Chapel Hill: University of North Carolina Press, 1958.

———. *Roanoke Island: The Beginning of English America.* Chapel Hill: University of North Carolina Press, 1984.

———, ed. *The Outer Banks Reader.* Chapel Hill: University of North Carolina Press, 1998.

Stratton, A. C. "Reclaiming the North Carolina Banks." *Shore and Beach* 11 (April 1943): 25–27, 32.

Stratton, A. C., and James R. Hollowell. *Methods of Sand Fixation and Beach Erosion Control.* Washington, D.C.: Department of the Interior, National Park Service, 1940.

"Ten Best Surf Towns in America." *Surfer* (July 2009). Available at http://surfermag .com/features/onlineexclusives/ten_best_surf_towns_in_america/index.html (accessed December 4, 2009).

Thieler, E. R., and E. S. Hammar-Klose. *National Assessment of Coastal Vulnerability to Future Sea-Level Rise: Preliminary Results for the U.S. Atlantic Coast.* U.S. Geological Survey. Open-File Report 99-593. 1999.

Thompson, Estes. "Oil Drilling Dispute Flares." *State* (Columbia, S.C.), June 19, 1998, F1.

Titus, James G. "Rising Seas, Coastal Erosion and the Takings Clause: How to Save Wetlands and Beaches without Hurting Property Owners." *Maryland Law Review* 57, no. 4 (1998): 1279–1399.

Trebanis, Arthur C., Orrin H. Pilkey, and Hugo R. Valverde. "Comparison of Beach Nourishment along the U.S. Atlantic, Great Lakes, Gulf of Mexico, and New England Shorelines." *Coastal Management* 27 (1999): 329–40.

Trefil, James. *A Scientist at the Seashore.* New York: Scribner, 1984.

Trenberth, K. E. "Warmer Oceans, Stronger Hurricanes." *Scientific American,* July 2007, 45–51.

U.S. Army Inspector General. "Report of Investigation." Case 00-019. 2000.

U.S. Commission on Ocean Policy. *An Ocean Blueprint for the 21st Century.* Washington, D.C., 2004.

Valverde, Hugo R., Arthur C. Trembanis, and Orrin H. Pilkey. "Summary of Beach Nourishment Episodes on the U.S. East Coast Barrier Islands." *Journal of Coastal Research* 15, no. 4 (1999): 1100–18.

Whitehead, John C. "One Million Dollars per Mile? The Opportunity Costs of Hurricane Evacuation." *Ocean and Coastal Management* 46 (2003): 1069–83.

Whitehead, John C., Ben Poulter, Christopher F. Dumas, and Okmyung Bin. "Measuring the Impacts of Sea Level Rise on Marine Recreational Shore Fishing in North Carolina." G2008. Available at http://ideas.repec.org/p/apl/wpaper/08-09 .html (accessed January 20, 2010).

Whitlock, C. "Flooded with Generosity." *Raleigh News and Observer,* November 17, 1997, 16.

Wirth, Conrad L. "A Letter to the People of the Outer Banks." *Coastland Times,* October 31, 1952, 5.

Young, Rob, and Andy Coburn. "Sandbag Seawalls Do More Harm than Good." *Topsail Voice,* June 11, 2008. Available at http://ncass.wcu.edu/WebFiles/PDFs/ Topsail_Voice_June_08.pdf (accessed December 5, 2009).

Zebrowski, Ernest. *Perils of a Restless Planet.* New York: Cambridge University Press, 1997.

Index

About the Author and the Photograp

JEFFREY POMPE is a professor of economics at
in Florence, South Carolina, where he is the N
fessor of Business and University Trustee Res
author of *Environmental Conflict: In Search of*

KATHLEEN POMPE is a professor of art at Francis
past thirty years her photography has been exh
person, invitational, and juried art shows throug
addition her photographs have appeared in man